BIBLE COLORING BOOK

Drawings by Cynthia McBrayer
Adapted from Illustrations in *Show Me Jesus* Curriculum

Guidelines for Copying

You MAY legally make photocopies of the coloring and activity pages in this book if:

- you or someone in your organization purchased this book
- the page is marked "OK to photocopy"
- the copies are for noncommercial use in your home, local church, or Christian ministry

You MAY NOT make photocopies if:

- you distribute them digitally (online or via e-mail)
- you use them in another product for sale
- you or your organization is not the original purchaser of this book
- you are sharing them with another church, organization, or family

Thank you for helping GCP serve the church!

GREAT COMMISSION PUBLICATIONS

 The *God's Story Bible Coloring Book* coordinates with Toddler, Preschool, and Younger Elementary *Show Me Jesus* curriculum. *Show Me Jesus* is a complete plan for nurturing children in the Word of God. Individual courses for ages two through high school fit together to teach the Bible as a whole and the unfolding story of redemption in Christ. The curriculum is rooted in our Reformed heritage and doctrine as embodied in the Westminster Standards.

Scripture quotations are from The Holy Bible, English Standard Version® (ESV®), copyright © 2001 by Crossway, a publishing ministry of Good News Publishers. Used by permission. All rights reserved.

Cover/text graphic design by Cynthia McBrayer

Copyright © 2010 by Great Commission Publications, Inc.

Second Printing 2014

Third Printing 2016

Permission is granted to reproduce pages in this book according to the guidelines on page 1.

Printed in the United States of America

Executive Director, Thomas R. Patete

Director of Publications, Mark L. Lowrey, Jr.

Production Manager, Donna Williams

Assistant Production Manager, Heather Cossar

Project Editor and Writer, Anna Trimiew

Art Director, Cynthia McBrayer

Theological Editor, William H. Smith

Drawings by Cynthia McBrayer
Adapted from Illustrations in *Show Me Jesus* Curriculum
Toddler: Drew Rose
Preschool: Keith Neely, Jack Brouwer (with additional illustrations by Unada Gliewe, Jack Kershner, Ed Olson, and Christine Patete)
Younger Elementary: Keith Neely, Jack Brouwer (with additional illustrations by Roman Dunets)

The signs and their descriptions found in this book have been taken with permission from
The Joy of Signing by Dr. Lottie L. Riekehof (Gospel Publishing House, 1987).

GREAT COMMISSION
PUBLICATIONS

3640 Windsor Park Drive
Suwanee, GA 30024-3897
800-695-3387 • www.gcp.org

Great Commission Publications is the joint publishing ministry of the
Committee on Christian Education of the Orthodox Presbyterian Church and the
Committee on Discipleship Ministries of the Presbyterian Church in America.

TABLE OF CONTENTS

Introduction 7
Coloring and Activity Pages 11

Toddler Curriculum Scope & Sequence Index 327
Preschool Curriculum Scope & Sequence Index 328
Younger Elementary Curriculum Scope & Sequence Index 330
Bible Story Index 332

OLD TESTAMENT
Creation

Genesis 1:1	God made everything.	11
Genesis 1:16	God made the sun, moon, and stars.	13
Genesis 1:21	God made fish and birds.	15
Genesis 1:9–12, 24–25	God made land, plants, and animals.	17
Genesis 1:26–31	God made people.	19
Genesis 1:28	We can tend and keep God's world.	21
Genesis 2:1–3	God set apart the Sabbath day.	23

God's People from Adam to Joseph

Genesis 2:15–17	God made a covenant with Adam.	25
Genesis 3:1–6	Adam and Eve sinned.	27
Genesis 3:15	God promised to send the Savior.	29
Genesis 3:21	God gave Adam and Eve clothes.	31
Genesis 4:1–16	Cain killed Abel.	33
Genesis 4:25	God gave Adam and Eve a new son, Seth.	35
Genesis 6–9	God saved Noah and his family.	37
Genesis 12, 15, 17	God called Abraham.	39
Genesis 13–14, 18–19	Abraham let Lot choose the land he wanted.	41
Genesis 21:1–7	Isaac was born to Abraham and Sarah.	43
Genesis 22:1–19	God provided a sacrifice in Isaac's place.	45
Genesis 24	God gave Isaac a wife.	47
Genesis 25	Esau sold his birthright to Jacob for stew.	49
Genesis 28	God spoke to Jacob in a dream.	51
Genesis 37	Joseph's brothers sold him as a slave.	53
Genesis 39	Joseph told Potiphar's wife no.	55
Genesis 39–41	God was with Joseph in prison.	57
Genesis 42–50	God used Joseph to save his family.	59

God's Nation: Israelites

Exodus 1–2	God saved baby Moses.	61
Exodus 3–4	God spoke to Moses from a burning bush.	63
Exodus 5–6	Moses and Aaron spoke to Pharaoh.	65
Exodus 7–10	God sent 10 plagues on Egypt.	67
Exodus 11–12	God's people celebrated the first Passover.	69
Exodus 13–15	God parted the Red Sea.	71
Exodus 16	God provided manna in the wilderness.	73
Exodus 17:1–7	God told Moses to strike the rock to get water.	75

Exodus 17:8–16	God told Moses to hold up his arms to win the battle.	77
Exodus 19–20, 24	Moses received God's Ten Commandments.	79
Exodus 20:8	Keep the Lord's Day holy.	81
Exodus 32–34	Moses broke the tablets when he saw the golden calf idol.	83
Exodus 35–40	The Israelites worshiped God at the tabernacle.	85
Numbers 13–14	The spies brought grapes from the Promised Land.	87
Numbers 16–17	Moses and Aaron led the Israelites, who often rebelled.	89
Numbers 21:4–9	Moses lifted the bronze snake. Those who looked at it were healed.	91
Deuteronomy 31–34	Moses saw the Promised Land.	93
Joshua 3–4	God parted the Jordan River so the people could cross.	95
Joshua 6	God gave the Israelites victory at Jericho.	97
Joshua 10	God made the sun stand still while Joshua led the battle.	99
Judges 6–7	God gave Gideon a sign.	101
Judges 13–16	Samson trusted God to give him strength.	103
Ruth 1–4	Ruth and Naomi trusted God.	105

Kings and Prophets

1 Samuel 1–2	Hannah praised God for giving her a son, Samuel.	107
1 Samuel 3	Samuel heard God calling his name.	109
1 Samuel 2:12–4:18	Hophni and Phinehas did not honor God or obey their father.	111
1 Samuel 13	Samuel told King Saul he disobeyed God.	113
1 Samuel 16:1–13	Samuel anointed David as king.	115
1 Samuel 16	David, the shepherd boy, sang songs of praise to God.	117
1 Samuel 17	God gave David victory over Goliath.	119
1 Samuel 18	King Saul was jealous of David.	121
1 Samuel 26	King Saul tried to kill David, but later he blessed him.	123
2 Samuel 7	Nathan told King David about God's promise.	125
2 Samuel 11–12; Psalm 51	King David was sorry for his sin.	127
1 Kings 3, 10	The queen of Sheba visited King Solomon.	129
1 Kings 17	God provided food for Elijah.	131
1 Kings 18	God sent fire to the altar when Elijah prayed.	133
1 Kings 21	Elijah told King Ahab that he sinned.	135
2 Kings 5	Naaman washed in the river and was healed.	137
2 Kings 22–23	King Josiah read God's Word to the people.	139
2 Chronicles 14–15	King Asa obeyed God's Word.	141
2 Chronicles 22–24	King Joash repaired the temple.	143
Ezra 1, 3	God's people returned to Jerusalem and rebuilt the temple.	145
Ezra 7; Nehemiah 8–10	Ezra taught God's Word.	147
Esther 1–10	Esther asked King Xerxes to save God's people.	149
Psalm 100	"Make a joyful noise to the Lord, all the earth!"	151
Isaiah 40–53; Micah 5, 7	God's Word is about his Son.	153
Jeremiah 37–39	Jeremiah preached God's message.	155
Daniel 1	Daniel and his three friends were brought to the king.	157
Daniel 3	God protected Shadrach, Meshach, and Abednego.	159
Daniel 5	Daniel read the strange words on the wall.	161
Daniel 6	God protected Daniel from the lions.	163
Jonah 1–4	Jonah spent three days inside the big fish.	165
Micah 5:2	Micah said the Messiah would be born in Bethlehem.	167

NEW TESTAMENT

Jesus' Birth and Childhood

Matthew 1	Joseph believed the angel's message about Jesus.	169
Luke 1:26–56	Mary believed the good news!	171
Luke 1:5–25, 57–80	John the Baptist was born.	173
Luke 2:1–20	Jesus was born!	175
Luke 2:1–20	The shepherds heard the good news of Jesus' birth.	177
Luke 2:22–35	Simeon saw the Savior.	179
Matthew 2:1–23	Wise men went to worship Jesus.	181
Luke 2:41–52	Jesus went to the temple when he was 12 years old.	183

Jesus' Ministry, Teaching, and Miracles

Matthew 3	John told about Jesus.	185
Luke 4:1–13	Satan tempted Jesus 3 times.	187
Luke 4:14–30	The people of Nazareth rejected Jesus.	189
Luke 5:1–11	Jesus called his first disciples.	191
John 2:1–11	Jesus' first miracle: changing water into wine	193
John 3:1–21	Nicodemus visited Jesus at night.	195
John 4:1–42	The woman at the well learned about living water from Jesus.	197
Matthew 5:43–48	Love your enemies and pray for them.	199
Matthew 7:16–20	Good trees bear good fruit. Bad trees bear bad fruit.	201
Matthew 7:24–27	The wise man built his house on a rock.	203
Matthew 16:13–18	Peter said Jesus is the Christ, the Son of the living God.	205
Matthew 17:1–8	Jesus revealed his glory.	207
Matthew 18:21–35	The king forgave his servant who owed him a lot of money.	209
Matthew 19:16–30; Luke 21:1–3	The rich young man and poor widow	211
Mark 4:35–41	Jesus calmed the storm.	213
Mark 5:21–43	Jesus raised Jairus's daughter from the dead.	215
Mark 6:30–44	Jesus fed 5,000 people with only 5 loaves and 2 fish.	217
Mark 10:13–16	Parents brought their children to Jesus.	219
Mark 10:46–52	Jesus healed blind Bartimaeus.	221
Luke 5:17–26	Jesus healed a paralyzed man.	223
Luke 7:1–10	A soldier's servant was healed by Jesus.	225
Luke 7:11–17	Jesus raised a widow's son to life.	227
Luke 7:36–50	The forgiven woman believed Jesus.	229
Luke 9:1–6	Jesus sent out his 12 disciples.	231
Luke 10:25–37	The good Samaritan helped the hurt man.	233
Luke 10:38–42	Martha was upset that Mary did not help her.	235
Luke 11:1–4; Matthew 6:9–14	The disciples asked Jesus to teach them how to pray.	237
Luke 13:10–17	Jesus healed a crippled woman on the Sabbath.	239
Luke 15:1–7	The shepherd looked for his one lost sheep.	241
Luke 15:11–24	The prodigal son who ran away came home to his father.	243
John 5:1–15	Jesus healed a lame man at the pool.	245
John 8:12–59	Many people put their trust in Jesus.	247
John 10:1–18	Jesus cares for his people like a shepherd cares for his sheep.	249
Luke 17:11–19	Only one healed leper thanked Jesus.	251
John 11:1–44	Jesus brought Lazarus back to life.	253
John 12:1–8	Mary anointed Jesus with expensive perfume.	255
Luke 19:1–10	Zacchaeus climbed a tree to see Jesus.	257

Jesus' Crucifixion Week and Resurrection

Luke 19:28–38	The people waved palm branches to praise Jesus.	259
Mark 11:15–18	Jesus cleansed the temple.	261
John 13:1–17	Jesus washed the disciples' feet.	263
Luke 22:7–20	The disciples received the Lord's Supper.	265
John 14	The disciples listened as Jesus told them about the Holy Spirit.	267
Luke 22:39–53	Men came to arrest Jesus.	269
Matthew 26	Peter was sad that he denied Jesus three times.	271
Luke 23	Jesus died on the cross.	273
Luke 23:32–43	A dying criminal turned to Jesus.	275
Matthew 27:57–61	Joseph of Arimathea provided a tomb for Jesus' body.	277
Luke 24:1–12	Jesus is alive!	279
John 20:1–18	Mary Magdalene saw Jesus' empty tomb.	281
Luke 24:13–35	Two people talked to the risen Jesus as they walked to Emmaus.	283
Luke 24:36–49	The disciples saw the risen Jesus.	285
Luke 24:50–53	The disciples saw Jesus return to heaven.	287

The Church Grows

Acts 1–2	The disciples received the Holy Spirit at Pentecost.	289
Acts 1–2	The disciples obeyed Jesus' command to make disciples.	291
Acts 2:42–3:26	Through Christ's power, Peter and John healed a lame man.	293
Acts 4–5	Peter and John told everyone about Jesus.	295
Acts 6:1–7	The disciples chose seven godly men.	297
Acts 8:26–40	Philip explained God's Word.	299
Acts 9:36–42	Dorcas served the church by sewing clothes for the poor.	301
Acts 10	Peter told Cornelius to believe in Jesus.	303
Acts 11:19–30	Paul and Barnabas brought offerings to the Jerusalem church.	305
Acts 12:1–17	The church prayed for Peter while he was in prison.	307
Acts 13:1–3	The church sent out Paul and Barnabas as missionaries.	309
Acts 13–14	Paul and Barnabas preached the good news of Jesus.	311
Acts 16:11–15	Lydia believed Paul's gospel message about Jesus.	313
Acts 16:16–40	Paul and Silas sang and praised God in prison.	315
Acts 23:11–24	Paul's nephew warned of Paul's enemies.	317
2 Timothy 1:5	Timothy's mother and grandmother taught him God's Word.	319
James 1:19–25	James wrote, "Listen to God's Word and do what it says."	321
1 John 3–4	John wrote a letter to the church that said, "Love one another."	323
Revelation 21:1–4	God will make his creation new one day!	325

INTRODUCTION for Teachers and Parents

Your children will be delighted with the pages to color in the **God's Story Bible Coloring Book**. It contains 158 drawings and activities intended for their enjoyment and learning! Parents and teachers can use this book along with *Show Me Jesus* Sunday school curriculum or on its own.

☆ Reproducible
Every coloring and activity page is reproducible. You may make copies for local church or home use only. Digital distribution (e-mail or online) or sharing copies with another organization are not permitted (see details on page 1).

☆ Active
Besides coloring, you'll find plenty of activities on the back of each coloring page to keep your little ones engaged! We've included games, crafts, active discussions, and songs to help your learners explore Bible stories in a fun, hands-on way. We also offer five CDs and songbooks to add music to your coloring sessions! See page 10 for details and how to order.

☆ With *Show Me Jesus* Sunday School
Are you teaching Great Commission Publications' Toddler, Preschool, or Younger Elementary Sunday school curriculum? Every coloring and activity page in this book matches a lesson from these three departments of Sunday school. Simply find the lesson you are teaching and make copies for the children. See the department index, pages 327–331, for a list of matching stories.

☆ Flexible
You can use these pages with your 3- to 8-year-olds at various times:
- At home with parents
- In midweek and other church programs
- With Sunday school early arrivers to introduce them to the Bible story
- During Sunday school to enhance the lesson
- After Bible teaching in Sunday school to review
- During the second hour to recall Bible truths from class

Each coloring page includes a Scripture verse or passage to help you retell the Bible story, read God's Word to the children, and emphasize Bible truths and words through fun activities after they color. However you use this book, your children will learn about our triune God, his wonderful love, and what he has done to redeem his people through Christ!

HOW TO USE THIS BOOK

☆ Talk About the Picture
When you hand out a coloring page, talk about the Bible picture and let your children express ideas about it too. Use the guided discussion on the back, which turns coloring time into Bible-learning time!

☆ Choose Activities to Do
Read through the Bible-learning activities on the back of the coloring page you plan to use. Each activity provides a way to expand on coloring time through a variety of talking, doing, making, and playing activities. Adapt activities to the age and developmental level of your children. You may choose to use only the coloring page, or to use just one or two activities on the back, depending on your group and time.

☆ Gather Supplies
Consider gathering the standard supplies listed below and putting them in a plastic tub labeled *God's Story Bible Coloring Book Supplies*. That way, you'll have what you need each time you use a coloring and activity page. Some activities require special supplies, which are indicated by **bold type** on each activity page. Locate and set aside the items you'll need ahead of time.

- ☐ **crayons**
- ☐ **washable markers**
- ☐ **colored pencils**
- ☐ **construction paper**
- ☐ **poster board**
- ☐ **transparent tape**
- ☐ **glue sticks**
- ☐ **safety scissors**
- ☐ **glitter glue**
- ☐ **play dough**

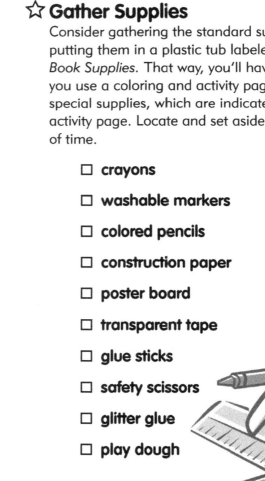

WHAT ARE THEY LIKE?

Toddlers, preschoolers, and younger elementary children are at various developmental levels with coloring skills. Twos and threes typically scribble outside the lines, usually with one color. Fours and fives often color outside the lines, sometimes with just one crayon or sometimes the whole box. Most first and second graders have mastered the art of coloring inside the lines and will finish quickly or be very detailed, depending on personality. For all ages, don't tell them how to color, which crayon to use, what part of the picture to fill in, and so forth. Let the children color as they like and genuinely appreciate their work and the way they do it.

☆ Toddlers (2- to 3-year-olds)
- have limited coloring/gluing skills
- are developing motor skills
- cannot think abstractly
- need simple and concrete examples
- are physically active
- follow simple directions
- know some Bible words
- have a growing but small vocabulary

☆ Preschoolers (4- to 5-year-olds)
- are developing small motor skills
- have increasing coloring skills; often color outside the lines
- are active learners who learn best from firsthand experiences
- love words, rhymes, and songs
- want to please
- have varying attention spans according to tasks
- like to listen to stories and conversations
- are talkative

☆ Younger Elementary Children
(6- to 8-year-olds)
- have mastered coloring skills
- are developing hand-eye coordination
- think in literal and concrete terms
- can follow specific instructions
- have difficulty sitting still for very long
- like all kinds of games
- are talkative
- enjoy Bible stories
- understand God's love through personal relationships

MUSIC FOR ALL AGES!

Great Commission Publications has songbooks and CDs to inspire children to praise the Lord through music. The activity pages in *God's Story Bible Coloring Book* suggest songs from these songbooks and CDs. They also coordinate with *Show Me Jesus* curriculum.

Toddler *Sing-Along With Me*
Songbook (item SS1155)
CD (item SS1156)

Preschool Volume 1
Songbook (item SS2155)
CD (item SS2156)

Preschool Volume 2
Songbook (item SS2255)
CD (item SS2256)

Younger Elementary Volume 1
Songbook (item SS3155)
CD (item SS3156)

Younger Elementary Volume 2
Songbook (item SS3255)
CD (item SS3256)

ORDER TODAY!

FREE curriculum samples also available
www.gcp.org or **800-695-3387**

Would you like to learn more about *Show Me Jesus*? Speak with our curriculum specialist at **877-300-8884**.

God made everything.
Genesis 1:1

☆Let's Talk

ASK God made the things in the picture. *Can you name some? What else did God make?*

SAY God made everything. He made everything by the power of his word. He spoke and the things he created appeared. When he looked at everything, he saw that it was very good. It was very good because God, our great and wonderful Creator, made it!

☆Let's Memorize

Invite everyone to sit in a circle. Go over questions 1–3 listed below. Ask the first question and have the children jump up and give the answer. Then have them sit down. Repeat the process with questions 2 and 3.

First Catechism Q/A 1–3

1 Q. *Who made you?*
A. **God.**

2 Q. *What else did God make?*
A. **God made all things.**

3 Q. *Why did God make you and all things?*
A. **For his own glory.**

☆Let's Thank God

Say this rhyme and have the children imitate you. Let them repeat each line after you and copy your actions.

Thank God for the shining sun, *(touch fingertips and make a circle overhead)*

Thank God for the busy bee, *(buzz like a bee)*

Thank God for all the animals, *(arms wide)*

Thank God for you and me! *(point to a friend, point to self)*

First Catechism teaches children Bible truths with 150 simple questions and answers.
www.gcp.org or 800-695-3387

Genesis 1

© GCP www.gcp.org
OK to photocopy for church and home use

God made the sun, moon, and stars.

Genesis 1:16

God made the sun, moon, and stars.
Genesis 1:16

☆Let's Talk

ASK *Why did God make the sun, moon, and stars?*

SAY God made the sun to give bright light during the daytime. He made the moon and stars to keep the night from being completely dark.

ASK *Who made day and night?*

SAY God made day and night as well as the sun, moon, and stars. God saw all that he had made. And he saw that it was good!

☆Let's Do

1. Give each child a sheet of **yellow construction paper** and a sheet of **black construction paper**. Explain that the yellow paper stands for daytime and the black paper stands for nighttime.

2. Tell the children that when you say something they might say during the day, they must hold up the yellow sheet and call out "Daytime!" When you say something they might say at night, they must hold up the black sheet and yell "Nighttime!"

3. Say each of the following sentences slowly and give your learners time to respond.

    "I just ate a good breakfast!" "Good night, Mom."

    "What did you bring for snack?" "It's time for t-ball practice!"

    "Let's listen to a bedtime story." "The school bell just rang."

    "Switch on the night-light, please." "Let's play outside."

☆Let's Pray

Lead your children in this prayer of thanks.

> Dear God, thank you for making the sun, moon, and stars. Thank you that we can work and play during the day and rest and sleep at night. Thank you for watching over us all through the daytime and nighttime. In Jesus' name, Amen.

Genesis 1

God made fish and birds.
Genesis 1:21

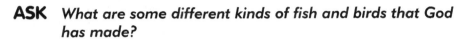

☆Let's Talk

ASK *What are some different kinds of fish and birds that God has made?*

SAY Each fish and bird is special and wonderfully made. God made dolphins that swim in the ocean and catfish that swim in the river. He made the beautiful eagle and the little chickadee.

ASK *What are some other creatures God has made? What do you know about them?*

SAY God made every creature for his own glory . . . for his praise!

☆Let's Make

Make a **photocopy** of the coloring page for each child. Mount each page on **poster board**. Have the children color the pictures. When they are finished, have them make touch-and-feel pictures. Lay out the following items and help the children **glue** them to their pictures: **rice, beans, glitter glue, cotton, tissue paper, yarn, fabric**.

☆Let's Rhyme

Say this rhyme and have the children imitate you.

God made the water. God made the sky,
(make wavy hand motions, then raise arms high and extend fingers)

God made the swishy fish swimming by.
(palms together, wiggle body)

God made the oceans. God made the air,
(make wavy hand motions, then breathe in and out deeply)

God made the birds that fly everywhere!
(wave arms up and down, pretend to fly around the room)

 **God made land, plants, and animals.**
Genesis 1:9–12, 24–25

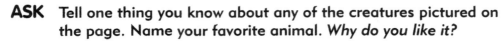

☆Let's Talk and Wonder

ASK Tell one thing you know about any of the creatures pictured on the page. Name your favorite animal. *Why do you like it?*

SAY God created everything and provided for everything he made. We know that everything God made is good and that all his works praise him!

SAY I wonder what the earth would be like if there was only one kind of plant and one kind of animal . . .

I wonder how we would feel if we didn't have cats and dogs for pets . . .

☆Let's Plan

Talk about the land, plants, and animals God has given us to care for and enjoy. Ask the children to name ways they can help take care of the things he's made. For example, they can plants seeds, water flowers, pick up trash, and feed the family pet.

☆Let's Praise

Choose one way to praise God for all his works and his care for all he has made.

SING a song about God's creation.

LISTEN to a song of praise on CD while coloring. Or the children can listen as you read aloud this page's Bible verses: Genesis 1:9–12, 24–25.

PRAY together, thanking God for making the earth, plants, and land animals. Ask him to help your students take care of the things he has made.

 GCP offers five CDs and songbooks designed specifically for children to praise God! See page 10 for details.

Genesis 1

© GCP www.gcp.org
OK to photocopy for church and home use

God made people.

Genesis 1:26–31

God made people.
Genesis 1:26–31

☆Let's Talk

ASK *Who are the first people God made? Who are the people in the picture?*

SAY God made Adam and Eve. He made them different from all the other creatures. God made man and woman in his image. That means God made them to be like him in some ways. God blessed Adam and Eve and told them to take care of the earth and to use it for food.

ASK *What are the names of some people you know?*

SAY God made every person in the world! He made us to trust and obey him and take care of what he has made. The Bible tells us to praise God. We glorify him when we love him and do what he says.

☆Let's Look

❶ Ahead of time, locate a **picture book** showing a variety of people and things God made. For example, look for pictures of children, families, animals, plants, trees, fruit, and so on.

❷ Gather the children around you. Turn to a picture from the book and hold it up. Ask the children to tell you what they see and say, **"God made . . . "** before naming the item. For example, a child might say, **"God made babies"** when looking at a picture of a baby.

☆Let's Sing

Lead the children in singing these words to the tune *London Bridge* as they march around the room and do actions.

Preschool Vol. 2 CD

God made people, yes he did, *(point to different people)*
Yes he did, yes he did. *(nod)*
God made people, yes he did, *(point to different people)*
Praise his name! *(clap)*

Genesis 1

© GCP www.gcp.org
OK to photocopy for church and home use

We can tend and keep God's world.

Genesis 1:28

We can tend and keep God's world.
Genesis 1:28

☆Let's Talk

ASK When God made Adam and Eve, he blessed them and told them to have many children. Then he gave them another special job. *What was it?*

SAY God told them to tend and keep the beautiful earth he had created. God wanted them to care for and use and manage what he had made in a way that honored him.

ASK *Whose job is it to water the plants in your house and take care of the pets?*

SAY When we tend and keep household plants and family pets, in some ways we are doing the work of caring for God's creation—the job God gave us to do. Everything we have comes from God. We enjoy what he has given us, and we can tend and keep it properly as he has asked us to do.

☆Let's Make

Ahead of time cut out **magazine pictures** of animals, plants, flowers, fruit, and people. Lay the pictures on the table. Place a sheet of **poster board** on the wall. Let the children **glue** the pictures on it to form a mural. Talk about ways people can tend and keep the animals, plants, and other things pictured in the mural.

☆Let's Play

Play this version of *Simon Says*. Say each command and have your followers do the actions. Use the game to help teach what it means to care for God's earth.

- *Simon says* bend down low and plant seedlings in the garden.
- *Simon says* run and get the watering can to water the seedlings.
- *Simon says* reach up high and switch off the light.
- *Simon says* turn around and give the dog a treat.
- *Simon says* stand on tiptoes to pet the sleeping kitten on the bookcase.

Genesis 1

© GCP www.gcp.org
OK to photocopy for church and home use

God set apart the Sabbath day.
Genesis 2:1–3

☆Let's Talk and Wonder

ASK *Why did God set apart the Sabbath day?*

SAY After God completed his work of making the world, he rested on the seventh day of creation. He made this day the Sabbath. God set apart the Sabbath day to remind his people to worship him as their Creator, Lord, and Savior. Before Jesus came, God's people celebrated the Sabbath on the seventh day of the week, which would be our Saturday.

ASK We now celebrate the Sabbath on Sunday, the Lord's Day. *Do you know why?*

SAY Jesus, our Savior, rose from the dead on Sunday, the first day of the week, so we now celebrate the Sabbath on Sunday. This is the day for God's people all over the world to rest and worship him.

☆Let's Do

1. Ahead of time, cut out paper hearts from **red construction paper**, one for each child.
2. Let the children gather in a circle. Lay the paper hearts on the floor in the middle of the circle.
3. The children will take turns to pick up a paper heart. As they hold it up, they will name one way they can show they love God by keeping the Sabbath. Examples of answers: resting, hearing God's Word, praying, singing songs of praise to him, doing good to others, and so on.

☆Let's Pretend

Look at the coloring picture. Lead the children in pretending to be some things represented there. They can be Adam and Eve resting in the garden. They can pretend to be different animals. They can eat grass, drink water, or take a nap. The children can pretend to be flowers and trees God made or birds flying in the gentle wind.

Genesis 2

© GCP www.gcp.org
OK to photocopy for church and home use

God made a covenant with Adam.
Genesis 2:15–17

☆Let's Talk

ASK *What does the coloring picture show? Do you remember what God said about the trees in the Garden of Eden?*

SAY God told Adam he could eat from any tree in the garden. But he must not eat from the tree of the knowledge of good and evil. *What did God call for and what did God promise in the covenant he made with Adam?* Let's find out!

☆Let's Say and Memorize

Gather in a circle. Go over the following questions and answers. Ask each question slowly and say its answer. Repeat the question and invite the children to repeat the answer with you.

First Catechism Q/A 23–27

23 Q. *What covenant did God make with Adam?*
A. **The covenant of life.**

24 Q. *What is a covenant?*
A. **A relationship that God establishes with us and guarantees by his word.**

25 Q. *In the covenant of life, what did God require Adam to do?*
A. **To obey God perfectly.**

26 Q. *What did God promise in the covenant of life?*
A. **To reward Adam with life if he obeyed God perfectly.**

27 Q. *What did God threaten in the covenant of life?*
A. **To punish Adam with death if he disobeyed God.**

☆Let's Worship

God loved Adam and Eve very much. He provided more than enough for them to enjoy and use in the garden home he gave them. If weather permits, take the children outside to look at God's creation firsthand. Point out various things he made, such as trees, flowers, and grass. Make a worship statement, such as **"We praise God for making trees."** Let each child make a worship statement about something he or she sees that God made.

☆Let's Sing

Lead the children in singing this song to the tune *The Farmer in the Dell*.

 *Preschool Vol. 2 CD*

God gives me what I need
To trust him and obey.
I can depend on him,
He'll help me every day!

Genesis 2

© GCP www.gcp.org
OK to photocopy for church and home use

Adam and Eve sinned.
Genesis 3:1–6

☆Let's Talk

Use questions 28, 33–35 to go over important Bible truths from Genesis 3 with the children.

First Catechism Q/A 28, 33–35

 Q. *Did Adam keep the covenant of life?*
A. No. He sinned against God.

 Q. *What was the sin of our first parents?*
A. Eating the forbidden fruit.

 Q. *Who tempted Adam and Eve to this sin?*
A. Satan tempted Eve first, and then he used her to tempt Adam.

 Q. *How did Adam and Eve change when they sinned?*
A. Instead of being holy and happy, they became sinful and miserable.

SAY Adam acted for all of us when he broke God's covenant. Adam's sin made us sinners as well. We cannot obey God because our hearts are spoiled by sin. Satan tempts us to disobey and we listen to him instead of God. The good news is that God sent his own Son to be our Savior from sin. God calls us to put our trust in Jesus Christ, the only One who can forgive our sins, make our hearts new, and make us right with God.

☆Let's Make

Get some **play dough**. Sit with your children and lead them in making shapes and forms from the story of Adam and Eve sinning. The children can make a tree, fruit, Adam, Eve, and so on. As they work, talk about what they are making.

☆Let's Sing

Lead the children in singing "Adam in the Garden." As you sing the first verse, pretend to hide in the garden like Adam. On the second verse, the children may cup their ears with their hands as they sing about listening to God speak.

 *Preschool Vol. 1* CD Songbook, p. 10

☆Let's Pray

Lead the children in saying this prayer, repeating after you phrase by phrase.

Dear God, I ask you to forgive my sins. Please help me to do what is right when I am tempted to do what is wrong. Thank you for sending Jesus to pay for all my sins. Help me to trust and obey you. In Jesus' name, Amen.

God promised to send the Savior.

Genesis 3:15

God promised to send the Savior.
Genesis 3:15

☆Let's Talk and Wonder

SAY God told Adam and Eve that one day he would send a special baby who would grow up and undo all the wrong Satan had done. Then God sent Adam and Eve out of the garden. He placed angels and a sword of fire to keep them away from the tree of life. His promise to send the Savior is written in his Word, the Bible.

ASK *Who was the baby God sent? How did he keep God's promise?*

SAY Many years later God sent his Son, Jesus, to earth to be the Savior of his people. Jesus grew from a baby into a man. He always trusted and obeyed God perfectly. Then he went to the cross and took the punishment we deserve for our sins. Jesus paid for the sins of Adam and Eve and for all God's people when he gave his life for us. Then God made Jesus alive again. One day, everyone who trusts in Jesus will live with him forever in heaven!

☆Let's Do

Place a large sheet of **paper** on the wall. Draw an outline of a cross on the paper. Have **praise stickers** available. Let the children take turns placing a sticker on the cross. As they fill the cross with stickers, let them name one thing about Jesus they can be thankful for. For example, **"I can be thankful that Jesus is God's Son"** or **"I can be thankful that baby Jesus came"** and so on.

☆Let's Make

Make wristbands. Cut out **cardboard** hearts, one for each child. Print the words *Jesus loves me* on each heart, leaving room for children to draw and color a cross. Using a **hole puncher,** make a hole in the heart and attach a length of **yarn** that fits around the child's wrist. Let each child wear his or her wristband and be ready to tell anyone who asks what Jesus did on the cross for his people!

God gave Adam and Eve clothes.
Genesis 3:21

☆ Let's Talk and Memorize

ASK Look at the picture. *How did God show his love for Adam and Eve after they sinned? Whom did God promise to send to save his people?*

SAY God showed his care by clothing Adam and Eve in animal skins to protect them. Even more important, he promised to take care of their sin by sending a Savior to pay for the sins of all God's people.

Use the questions and answers below to go over Bible truths from Genesis 3 with your children.

First Catechism Q/A 37, 45–46

37 Q. *What effect did the sin of Adam have on you and all people?*
A. We are all born guilty and sinful.

45 Q. *How did you break the covenant of life?*
A. Adam represented all people, and so I fell with Adam in his first sin.

46 Q. *How, then, can you be saved?*
A. By the **Lord Jesus Christ** through the **covenant of grace**.

☆ Let's Snack

Enjoy a fruit snack together! Gather **apple slices, grapes, or another fruit**. As you eat, ask: What color is the fruit? Is the skin smooth or rough or fuzzy? What did God say about one kind of tree in the Garden of Eden? What happened when Adam and Eve ate from it?

☆ Let's Rhyme

Lead the children in this rhyme. They can repeat what you say and copy what you do.

God reached out to me in love, *(cross hands over heart)*
The Savior came from heaven above. *(use both arms to form a cross)*
I will trust him and obey, *(fold hands as if in prayer)*
Because he cares for me each day! *(draw large heart shape with both index fingers)*

☆ Let's Pray

Ask children to close their eyes and repeat each phrase of this prayer after you.

Dear God, thank you that Jesus came to take care of our guilt and sin. Those who trust in him for forgiveness are no longer guilty before you. Thank you for loving me. In Jesus' name, Amen.

Genesis 3

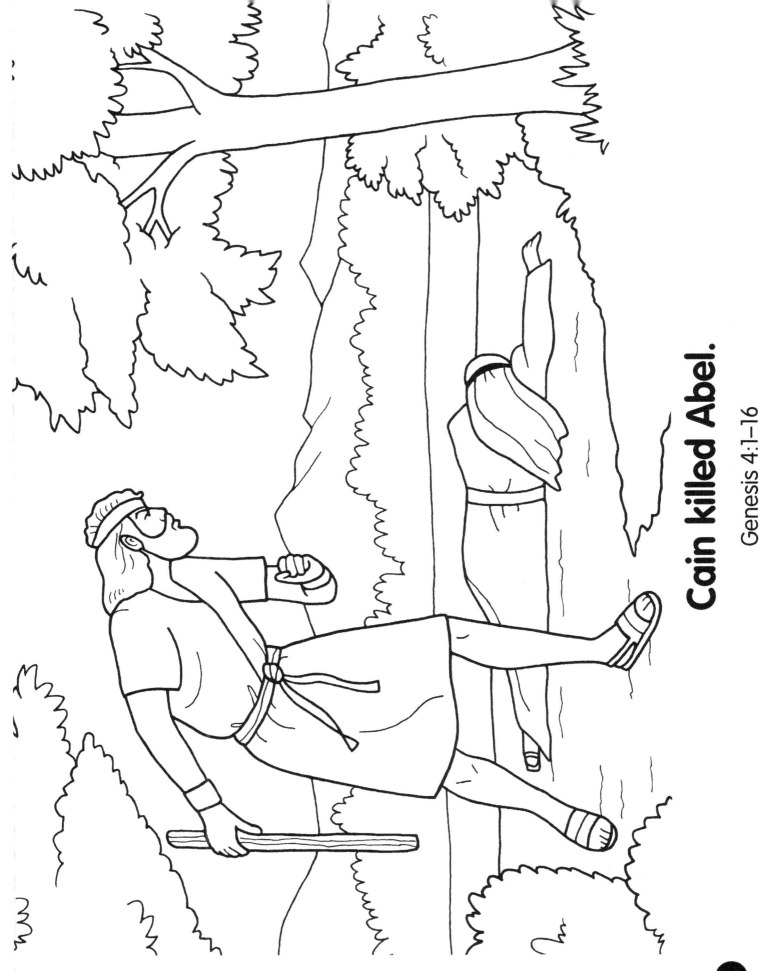

Cain killed Abel.
Genesis 4:1–16 (Exodus 20:13)

☆Let's Talk and Wonder

SAY The sixth commandment says, "You shall not murder." It teaches us to love and protect human life. God wants us to be kind and care for others so that the seeds of murder—anger, jealousy, and hatred—will not have room to grow in our hearts and minds.

ASK Look at the picture of Cain and Abel. *What do you see?*

SAY Cain was jealous and upset with Abel because God accepted Abel's offering but rejected Cain's. In his anger, Cain attacked Abel in the field and killed him.

ASK *What did God do?*

SAY God punished Cain, but he promised to spare his life. God put a warning sign on Cain. It was a mark to tell others to keep away from Cain and not kill him.

SAY I wonder if everyone has broken the sixth commandment . . .

SAY We *all* have broken the sixth commandment because we don't love others as we love ourselves. Because of our sin we cannot obey God's commandments perfectly. But when we trust the Lord Jesus as our Savior, he forgives our sin and gives us the power we need to obey God's Word!

☆Let's Make and Do

Give each child **two index cards**. Have the children draw a heart on one card and a sad face on the other card. Explain that if you tell about something that pleases God, the children must hold up the card with the heart. If it is something that does not please God, they must hold up the card with the sad face. Give children time to respond to each one before moving on to the next.

- Josh is always mean to Jack because Josh is jealous of Jack.
- Nobody likes Laura. But even so, Ann asked Laura to sit with her at lunch.
- Eric was being a bully in recess. So Peter prayed for him that night.
- Sally took Heather's pencil and lost it. Heather forgave Sally.
- Billy tripped Caleb on purpose. When Caleb got up, he punched Billy in the nose.
- Tim treated Aaron badly. But Aaron invited Tim to church, and they became friends.

☆Let's Pray

Gather in a circle, holding hands. Ask God to help us please him by showing love to others, especially when it is hard to do so.

God gave Adam and Eve a new son, Seth.

Genesis 4:25

God gave Adam and Eve a new son, Seth.
Genesis 4:25

☆Let's Talk

ASK Adam and Eve sinned against God. But God made a promise to take care of their sin. *What did God promise?*

SAY He promised to send a Savior. God had a wonderful plan to send someone many years later from Eve's family line who would pay for Adam and Eve's sin and the sin of all God's people.

SAY First, God gave Adam and Eve two sons, Cain and Abel. Abel trusted God, but Cain did not. Cain killed Abel.

ASK Some time later, God gave Adam and Eve a new son. *What was his name?*

SAY God gave Adam and Eve a new son named Seth. Many years later, Jesus, God's promised Savior, was born into Seth's family line. God always keeps his promises!

☆Let's Sing and Do

Bring several **baby blankets or towels** to class. Give each child a blanket. Do these motions as you sing to the tune *Here We Go Round the Mulberry Bush*.

Preschool Vol. 2 CD

❶ God made a promise to Adam and Eve,
Adam and Eve, Adam and Eve.
God made a promise to Adam and Eve—
He promised to send a Savior!
(wave blanket overhead, like a praise banner)

❷ Adam and Eve had baby Seth,
Baby Seth, baby Seth.
Adam and Eve had baby Seth—
God would keep his promise!
(spread blanket, lay picture on it)

❸ Through Seth's family, Jesus came,
Jesus came, Jesus came.
Through Seth's family, Jesus came—
Jesus is the Savior!
(bundle blanket, rock gently)

❹ We believe God's promises,
God's promises, God's promises,
We believe God's promises—
He always keeps his Word!
(fold blanket, hold open like a book)

☆Let's Pray

Gather for prayer. Ask children to repeat this prayer after you, sentence by sentence.

Dear God, thank you for your promise of a Savior. Thank you for sending Jesus to be our Savior. Thank you that you always keep your promises. Please help us to trust in you more. In Jesus' name, Amen.

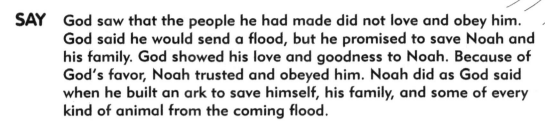

God saved Noah and his family.
Genesis 6–9

☆Let's Talk

SAY God saw that the people he had made did not love and obey him. God said he would send a flood, but he promised to save Noah and his family. God showed his love and goodness to Noah. Because of God's favor, Noah trusted and obeyed him. Noah did as God said when he built an ark to save himself, his family, and some of every kind of animal from the coming flood.

ASK *What happened after the flood?*

SAY When Noah, his family, and the animals left the ark for dry land, Noah offered a sacrifice and worshiped God. He praised God for taking care of them.

ASK God made another promise to Noah. *What was it?*

SAY God promised never again to destroy the earth with a flood. God sent a rainbow as a sign that he would keep his promise.

☆Let's Play

1. Play *All Aboard!* Gather **pictures of animals** whose sounds are easily made by children (dog, cat, duck, pig, cow, etc.). Put the pictures in a **bag**. Mark off an ark-shaped area on the floor with **masking tape**. Have children gather in pairs at the other end of the room.
2. Have all the pairs pick a card, look at the picture, and then put it facedown. At your signal, all the pairs will crawl or "fly" as fast as they can to the "ark" while making their animals' sounds. The first pair there is the winner!
3. Once inside the ark, have each pair take turns making the sound of their animal while the rest of the children guess what kind of animal they are.

☆Let's Draw

Hand out **paper** and **crayons** for the children to draw and color a rainbow of promise.

☆Let's Pray

Dear God, thank you for watching over me all the time. Thank you for your faithful care and for keeping your promises. Help me to trust you and obey. In Jesus' name, Amen.

God called Abraham.
Genesis 12, 15, 17

☆ Let's Talk and Wonder

SAY God told Abraham to leave his country and move to a new land that God would show him. God promised to bless Abraham with children and make him a great nation. Abraham trusted and obeyed God. He and his wife, Sarah, packed up their belongings and moved to Canaan, the new home God gave them.

ASK Later on, God took Abraham outside at night and showed him the stars. *Why?*

SAY God told Abraham to count the stars. But, of course, he couldn't count them all! God told Abraham that so many people would come from his children and grandchildren that no one would be able to count them, just like the stars in the sky! God promised Abraham and Sarah, who were very old, that they would have a baby boy. Abraham believed God. The Lord gave him faith to follow him and believe his promises.

SAY I wonder how Abraham and Sarah felt on their way to the new land God had promised them . . .

I wonder what Abraham thought when he heard God's promise . . .

☆ Let's Make

Give each child a sheet of **paper** and **crayons**. Tell the children they are going to make pictures of someone like Abraham who wants to trust and obey God—and that someone is *themselves!* As they work, go around the room and talk to the children about belonging to God and trusting him. Add this caption to each drawing:
God helps (name of child) **trust and obey him.**

☆ Let's Listen and Look

If possible, locate and bring to class the storybook *Count the Stars! The Story of God's Promise to Abraham and Sarah* by Patricia Nederveld. Read it aloud to your children. They will enjoy listening to the words and looking at the pictures!

☆ Let's Sing

Sing "Praise Him, Praise Him." Remind children that we belong to a wonderful, caring God and we want to praise, love, thank, and serve him!

Preschool Vol. 1 CD (track 19)
Songbook, p. 26

Genesis 12, 15, 17

© GCP www.gcp.org
OK to photocopy for church and home use

Abraham let Lot choose the land he wanted.

Genesis 13–14, 18–19

Abraham let Lot choose the land he wanted.
Genesis 13–14, 18–19

☆ Let's Talk

SAY Abraham and his nephew Lot had been traveling together, but it was time for them to settle and live in different parts of Canaan. Abraham let Lot look at the land and make his choice first.

ASK Look at the picture. *Who do you see?*

SAY Lot chose to live on the flat, grassy land next to the Jordan River. That part of the land included a city called Sodom, which was very wicked. That left the hilly, rocky part of the land for Abraham.

SAY Some time later, God told Abraham he would destroy the wicked cities in Lot's part of the land. Abraham prayed and asked God to spare the cities, if possible, for the sake of God's people who might be living in them. God answered his prayer, not by sparing the cities but by showing mercy to Lot and his family. God told Lot and his family to leave Sodom and not look back.

ASK *Do you know if everyone in Lot's family obeyed God's command?*

SAY Lot's wife looked back and God punished her. When Lot and his daughters were safe, God destroyed the wicked cities. The next day, Abraham looked across the plain of the Jordan River. All he could see was the thick smoke coming up from the burned ruins. God had remembered Abraham and saved Lot.

☆ Let's Play and Say

1. Cut out a heart from **red construction paper**.
2. Everyone sit in a circle. Play some **music** and pass the heart around the circle. Stop the music. Have the child holding the heart tell one way to show God's mercy and kindness to others (for example, playing with a lonely child on the playground, helping mom when she's busy, and so on). Start the music again and continue playing until every child has named a way to show God's mercy and kindness.
3. Remind children that God showed his mercy toward all his people when he sent Jesus to die for their sins.

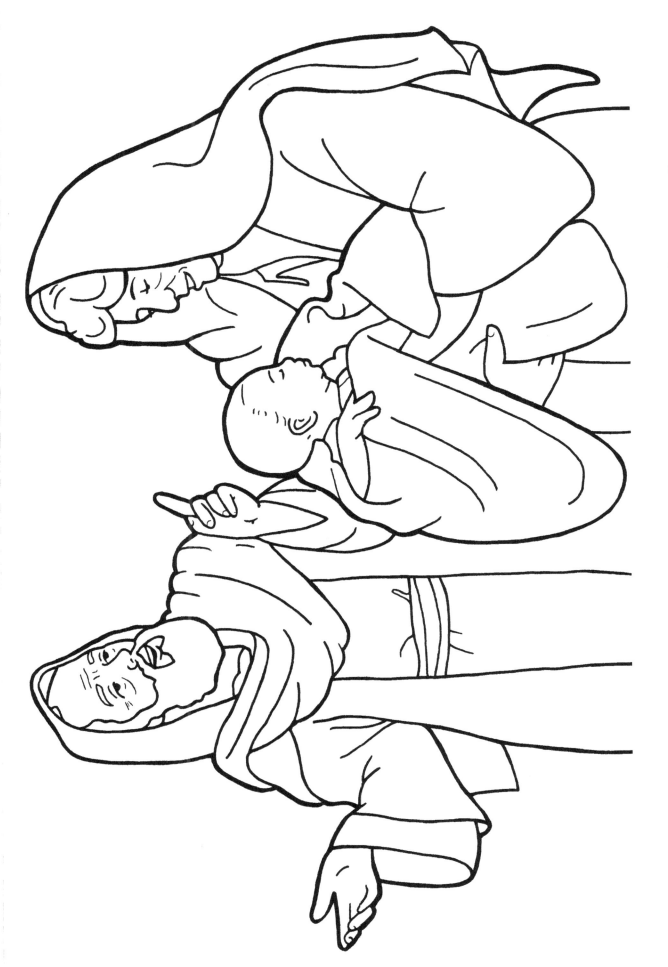

Isaac was born to Abraham and Sarah.
Genesis 21:1–7

 **Isaac was born to Abraham and Sarah.**
Genesis 21:1–7

☆Let's Talk

ASK *What do you see in the picture?*

SAY Just as God promised, a baby boy was born to Abraham and Sarah in their old age. They named him Isaac.

ASK *How do you think they felt when baby Isaac was born?*

SAY Sarah laughed with joy and thankfulness. Before, Sarah had not believed God's promise. Now she trusted God. She knew that nothing is too hard for God. As Sarah and Abraham looked at their precious child, they praised God for keeping his promises to them.

☆Let's Act

Bring in **simple Bible-times costumes, a doll,** and **baby blanket.** Have the children dress up and act out the story of Isaac's coming, based on the Scriptures listed above, as you tell it simply and actively. Choose children to be Abraham and Sarah and have the doll represent baby Isaac.

☆Let's Make

Write in block letters **God Loves to Help and Bless His Children** on a large sheet of **poster board.** Pass out **name tags** and have children print their names, with your assistance if needed. Then hand out **gold star stickers** so children can decorate and personalize the name tags. Children can arrange and attach their "starry" name tags to the poster around the words. Say the caption together a few times.

☆Let's Pray

Invite the children to bow their heads and close their eyes. Have them repeat this prayer after you, line by line.

> Dear God, thank you that you always keep your promises.
> Nothing is too hard for our great and wonderful God.
> We are helpless without you.
> Help us to trust in you, depend on you, and obey you.
> In Jesus' name, Amen.

God provided a sacrifice in Isaac's place.
Genesis 22:1–19

☆Let's Talk

SAY Abraham and Sarah loved their son, Isaac, very much. They taught him to pray and believe in God's promises. Isaac learned to trust and obey God. Then one day God tested Abraham.

ASK *What did God tell Abraham to do?*

SAY God told Abraham to take Isaac to a mountain and offer him there as a sacrifice. People usually gave lambs or other animals to God for their offerings. But God was asking Abraham to give his own dear son Isaac!

SAY Abraham trusted in God and his promises. So Abraham obeyed God—even though it was hard to do so! He and Isaac went to the place where God had told him to go. Once there, God stopped him from sacrificing his son and provided a ram in Isaac's place, just as God provided Christ to take our place. How thankful Abraham and Isaac were that they belonged to God and that God provided all they needed—not only in life but for their eternal salvation.

☆Let's Make and Talk

❶ Remind your children that before Christ came, people showed they trusted and obeyed God by offering animal sacrifices for sin on an altar. They looked forward to the day when the promised Savior would come and save them from their sins. When Jesus came, he died in our place on the cross. God saves his people and provides all we need, and we can always count on him to help us trust and obey him.

❷ Cut out **gray paper** stones to make an altar and **brown paper** wooden beams to make a cross. Let children **glue** paper stones to a large sheet of **construction paper** to make an altar. Talk about how the altar reminds us that God provided a ram as a sacrifice in Isaac's place. Then paste the paper beams in the shape of a cross on top of the altar. The cross reminds us that Jesus was sacrificed for us.

❸ As they work, let children mention times when they and their families trusted and obeyed God, even though it was hard.

☆Let's Pray

Gather the children around you. Ask God to give each child a heart that desires to trust, obey, and follow the Savior, even when it may be hard to do so! Thank God for providing Jesus as the sacrifice for sin.

 **God gave Isaac a wife.**
Genesis 24

☆Let's Talk

SAY God had promised Abraham many descendants. Abraham told his servant to go far away to the place where he used to live to get a wife for Isaac, his son.

ASK *What do you think the servant did?*

SAY The servant went to Abraham's homeland. He stopped by a well and prayed that God would help him choose the right girl for Isaac. God heard his prayer. A beautiful girl named Rebekah came to the well.

ASK *What do you think happened next?*

SAY Rebekah gave the servant and his camels water to drink. In turn, the servant gave her a necklace and ring. The servant went to Rebekah's house and her family said she could go off and marry Isaac.

ASK *What do you see in the picture?*

SAY The servant took Rebekah back to Isaac. He loved the girl God had chosen to be his wife. Isaac and Rebekah got married. God had provided a wife for Isaac so God's promises to Abraham would be fulfilled!

☆Let's Sing and Move

Sing these words to the tune *The Farmer in the Dell*. Children can clap or do other motions as they sing all seven verses:

 *Preschool Vol. 2* CD

1. Isaac needed a wife,
   Isaac needed a wife,
   Hi-ho the derry-o,
   Isaac needed a wife.

More verses:
2. The servant went away . . .
3. Rebekah came to the well . . .
4. The servant brought her back . . .
5. Isaac loved Rebekah . . .
6. They got married . . .
7. God answers prayer . . .

☆Let's Freeze and Say

God not only provided for Isaac; he provides all good things for us as well. Play this game to think about God's provision. Play **praise music** while children march around the room. Stop the music and have the children freeze. Call on a child to name one good thing God has provided for her family. Start the music, march, and then stop and freeze again. Give everyone a chance to name a good thing God gives his children.

Genesis 24

© GCP www.gcp.org
OK to photocopy for church and home use

Esau sold his birthright to Jacob for stew.

Genesis 25

Esau sold his birthright to Jacob for stew.
Genesis 25

☆Let's Talk

SAY Many years after Isaac and Rebekah were married, God gave them twin sons. When the boys were born, they did not look alike. Esau, the firstborn son, had hairy skin. The younger twin, Jacob, had smooth skin.

SAY When the boys grew up, they acted differently, too. Esau hunted. Jacob lived quietly, staying close to home. One day, when Esau came home very hungry, he saw that Jacob had made some lentil stew. "Quick," he said to Jacob, "let me have some of that stew!"

ASK Look at the picture. *What do you see?*

SAY First, Jacob made Esau promise to give him the birthright, that is, the blessing, gifts, and promises Esau would get for being the oldest son in the family.

ASK *What do you think Esau did?*

SAY Esau didn't care about God's promises to his family. He wanted something to eat right then! So he carelessly traded his birthright to Jacob for a bowl of lentil stew. But God was at work. God had said that his promises would be inherited by Jacob. So even though Esau did not care for God's promises like he should have, God was working out his plan to fulfill his promises through Jacob.

☆Let's Make

Use **colored construction paper** to cut out large shapes that look like bowls. Bring in **magazine pictures of food**. Help the children cut out pictures of their favorite foods and paste them onto their bowls to make their very own "stew." As they work, talk about the things they like to eat!

☆Let's Pray and Sing

❶ Have the children repeat this prayer after you, line by line.

Dear God, thank you for making us your people.
Please forgive our sins. Help us believe your promises.
Help us trust and obey you. In Jesus' name, Amen.

❷ Sing "God Is So Good."  *Toddler Sing-Along With Me* CD
Songbook, p. 9

Genesis 25

© GCP www.gcp.org
OK to photocopy for church and home use

God spoke to Jacob in a dream.

Genesis 28

God spoke to Jacob in a dream.
Genesis 28

☆Let's Talk

ASK *What do you see in the picture? What else?*

SAY While Jacob slept outdoors, with his head on a stone for a pillow, he had a dream.

ASK *What did Jacob dream?*

SAY Jacob dreamt that there was a stairway reaching to heaven, with angels going up and down the stairway. God was standing there, and he told Jacob that he was the God of Abraham and Isaac. He promised to give Jacob, the son of Isaac and Rebekah, the land where he was sleeping, and said he would bless him with many children. God promised to be with Jacob, watch over him always, and keep all his promises to him!

ASK *When Jacob woke up, what did he promise to do?*

SAY Jacob made a promise to serve and worship God. And even though Jacob did not trust and obey God perfectly, God always cared for Jacob and blessed him, just as he said he would!

☆Let's Play and Say

Use **masking tape** to mark off a large ladder-shaped area on the floor. Let children line up at one end of the ladder. They can take turns "climbing" the ladder by stepping on each taped rung. As they climb from one end to the other, remind children that God watches over them all the time. Have them name things they do or places they go where God is with them. They might say God watches over them when they play or God watches over them when they go to the store with mom and so on.

☆Let's Rhyme

Teach your children the following rhyme. Emphasize the syllables that are capitalized.

❶ God **WATCH**es Over **ME**,
EVery**WHERE** I **GO**.
WHEN I **REST** or **PLAY**—
He's **AL**ways **THERE, I KNOW!**

❷ God **WATCH**es Over **ME**,
EVery**WHERE** I **GO**.
I'll **TRUST** him **AND** o**BEY**—
He **CARES** for **ME, I KNOW!**

 **Joseph's brothers sold him as a slave.**
Genesis 37

☆Let's Talk

SAY God gave Jacob 12 sons. But Jacob loved his young son Joseph most of all and gave him a beautiful coat.

ASK *How do you think Joseph's older brothers felt when they saw what their father did for Joseph?*

SAY Joseph's older brothers were jealous of Joseph because their father loved him best. When they saw Joseph in his coat, they were very angry with him. One day they took their father's flocks to graze in fields some distance away. Jacob sent Joseph to find his brothers and see if they were safe.

SAY The brothers wanted to get rid of Joseph. So they grabbed him, ripped off his coat, and pushed him down an empty well.

ASK Look at the picture. *What happened next?*

SAY The brothers saw travelers passing by. They were riding their camels to a place far away. The brothers sold Joseph to the travelers, who took Joseph all the way to Egypt. Joseph became a slave in Egypt. It was very hard for young Joseph to be so far away from his family, but he was not alone. God was with Joseph all the time, caring for him, blessing his work, and using him to fulfill God's plan!

☆Let's Play Dress-Up

Gather **scarves, sashes, towels,** and **robes** to represent Bible-times clothing. Include a **colorful shirt or jacket** for Joseph's coat. Let children take turns dressing up as Joseph and his brothers. They can also dress up as travelers passing by, on their way to Egypt.

☆Let's Build and Say

Set out **building blocks**. Let the children build the deep, dark empty well where Joseph was thrown by his brothers. As they work, mention that God was with Joseph when he wore the coat. He was with Joseph when he was in the empty well. He was with Joseph when the travelers took him to Egypt. God was always with Joseph, and God is always with us, leading us and caring for us!

Joseph told Potiphar's wife no.
Genesis 39

Joseph told Potiphar's wife no.
Genesis 39 (Exodus 20:14)

☆Let's Talk

SAY Joseph worked hard for his master Potiphar in Egypt. Potiphar saw that the Lord was with Joseph in all that he did and put him in charge of his entire household.

SAY Potiphar's wife saw Joseph and wanted him to commit a sin. She grabbed his coat, but Joseph tore himself away, leaving his coat in her hand as he ran out of the house. He would not do as she asked; he would not sin against God. Joseph chose to be pure in his thoughts, words, and actions toward Potiphar's wife.

SAY Because Joseph resisted Potiphar's wife, she lied about him. She said that Joseph had been mean to her. Sadly, Potiphar believed his wife and put Joseph in prison to punish him.

ASK *What happened to Joseph?*

SAY God was in control of everything that happened to Joseph. The chief jailer saw that Joseph was a good man and put him charge of all the prisoners. After Joseph was allowed to leave prison, Joseph continued to trust and obey God. God was with Joseph and helped him think, say, and do the right thing!

☆Let's Think, Say, and Do

Use a **cardboard tube** for a pretend microphone. Announce that you are the host of a TV show called *Let's Think, Say, and Do the Right Thing*. Ask questions about thinking, saying, and doing things that are pleasing to the Lord in the daily lives of the children. For example, you might ask, **"When your sister won't share, what can you think, say, and do that is right?"** Then put the "microphone" in front of the child who wants to answer. Continue asking questions until all children have had an opportunity to be interviewed.

☆Let's Pray

Dear Lord Jesus, please teach us to hear, understand, and obey your Word, the Bible. Help us choose to be pure in our thoughts, words, and actions. Please forgive us when we sin. In your name we pray, Amen.

God was with Joseph in prison.

Genesis 39–41

God was with Joseph in prison.
Genesis 39–41

☆Let's Talk and Wonder

ASK Joseph, one of Jacob's 12 sons, was thrown in prison for something he did not do. *Can you name some of the other things that happened to Joseph?*

SAY Jacob loved Joseph and gave him a special coat. Joseph's brothers were angry and jealous. They threw him into a well and later sold him to some travelers who took Joseph to Egypt, where he was sold as a slave and later put into prison. While Joseph was in prison, the king of Egypt had a dream, and he sent for Joseph. Joseph explained what the dream meant. The king knew that God was with Joseph, and so he made Joseph the second most important ruler in Egypt.

ASK *Who was with Joseph when all these things happened?*

SAY God was with Joseph all the time and in every place. In every situation, Joseph trusted in God. He knew that God saved him, and that he was always there, guiding and helping him.

SAY I wonder how Joseph felt when his brothers were mean to him . . .

I wonder how Joseph felt when he was thrown in prison for something he didn't do . . .

I wonder how Joseph felt when he was made the second most important ruler in Egypt . . .

☆Let's Roll and Rhyme

Sit the children in a circle. Roll a **soft ball** to a child and lead the group in saying the following rhyme.

> Hello, children, this is what we'll do!
> We'll tell everyone—"God is with you!"

The child holding the ball points to someone in the circle, repeats **"God is with you!"** and then rolls the ball to the child. Repeat the rhyme and continue as before. The game continues until everyone has had a turn.

☆Let's Sing

Lead the class in singing "Praise the Lord." *Preschool Vol. 1* CD
Songbook, p. 27

Genesis 39–41

© GCP www.gcp.org
OK to photocopy for church and home use

God used Joseph to save his family.
Genesis 42–50

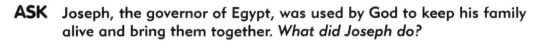

☆Let's Talk and Wonder

ASK Joseph, the governor of Egypt, was used by God to keep his family alive and bring them together. *What did Joseph do?*

SAY Joseph's 11 brothers and father, Jacob, did not have any food in Canaan. So some of his brothers came to Egypt to buy food. Joseph filled their bags with grain and sent them home. They came back for more food, and that time Joseph told them he was their brother. They were very sorry for treating him badly long ago. Joseph forgave his brothers. Then he sent them back home to bring their father, Jacob, and their families to live in Egypt. Now they would have plenty to eat, they would all be together, and God's plan to make his people into a great nation would continue, just as he had promised!

SAY I wonder how Joseph felt when he saw how God saved his entire family and brought them together in Egypt . . .

☆Let's Match and Make

1 Make one **photocopy** of the coloring page for each child. Cut the pictures in two, separating Joseph and his brothers. Put the pieces on the table in random order. Tell children that Joseph and his family were separated, like the pictures. Joseph lived in Egypt and his father and brothers lived in Canaan, the land God gave them.

2 Help children find both parts of the coloring page. When everyone has both parts of the picture, help them **tape** the two parts together so Joseph and his family come together. As children hold up their taped pictures, remind them that God saved Jacob's family and brought them together through Joseph.

3 Write the children's names on their taped pictures. Provide the following items for children to **glue** on the picture after they color it: **glitter glue**, **fabric**, and **stars**.

☆Let's Pray and Sing

Lead children in singing this prayer to the tune *Jesus Loves Me*. Sing each line and have children repeat after you.

Preschool Vol. 1 CD

> Thank you, God, for doing what's best,
> In your care, I'll always rest.
> Help me trust you, as I should,
> All you do is for my good!

After singing, end the prayer by saying: **In Jesus' name, Amen.**

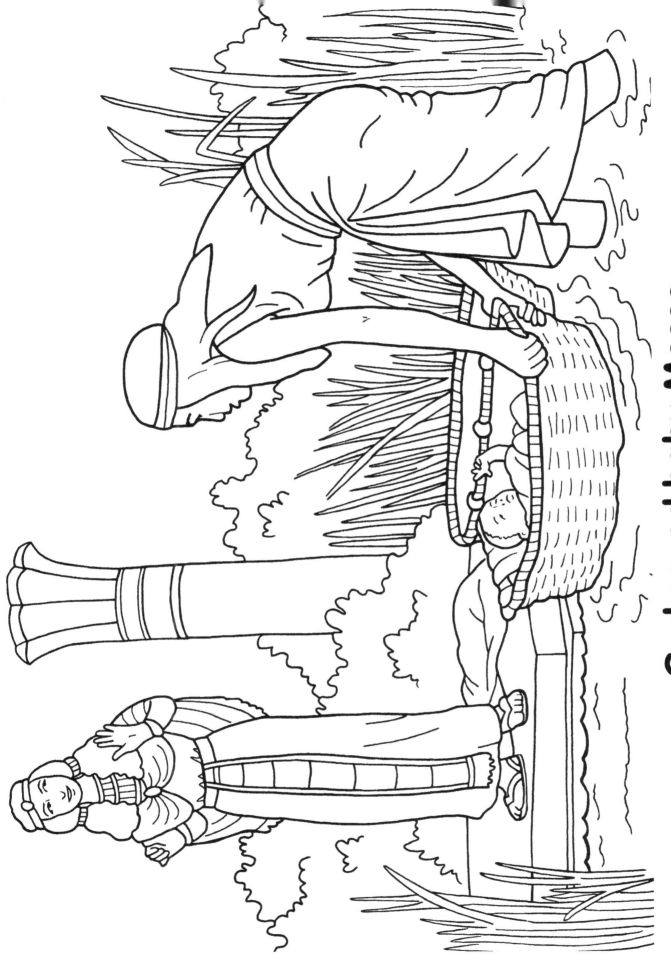

God saved baby Moses.
Exodus 1–2

☆Let's Talk

ASK *What do you see in the picture? What else?*

SAY Pharaoh was a very bad king. He gave an order that all Israelite baby boys must be killed. A fine baby boy was born to an Israelite family. The mother made a strong, safe basket. She put her baby in it and placed the basket among the reeds by the river, where he would be safe. The king's daughter went down to the river and saw the basket. She found the baby boy inside.

ASK *What happened when the princess found the Israelite baby?*

SAY The princess wanted to keep the baby as her own, but she needed someone to care for him. That someone was his very own family! She let him live with his family for a while and they taught him to love God. When he was older, he went to live with the princess in the palace. She named him Moses.

SAY God took care of baby Moses because God had a special job for him to do later on. God loves his people and always takes care of them.

☆Let's Make and Mention

Use **play dough** to make shapes representing a baby in a basket. Spend a few minutes talking about how God saves, cares for, and protects us today. Mention that God cares for us and is with us wherever we go and whatever we do. Remind the children that God sent Jesus to save us and forgive our sins.

☆Let's Sing

Sing together "God Is So Good." Teach children how to sign the second verse, "He cares for me." Then lead them in signing the words as they sing.

Preschool Vol. 2 CD
Songbook, p. 6

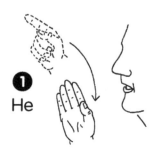
❶ He

❷ cares

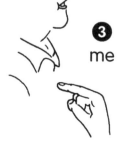
❸ me

❹ good

Sign illustrations from *The Joy of Signing* © 1987 Gospel Publishing House

God spoke to Moses from a burning bush.

Exodus 3–4

God spoke to Moses from a burning bush.
Exodus 3–4 (Exodus 20:7)

☆Let's Talk

SAY When Moses grew up, he went to a place called Midian and became a shepherd. One day he led his flock to a mountain in the desert.

ASK Look at the picture. *What does it show?*

SAY Moses saw that a bush was on fire but it did not burn up! God spoke to Moses from the burning bush. He told Moses he was sending him to Pharaoh, the king, to bring God's people, the Israelites, out of Egypt.

ASK *What did Moses say when he heard God's call?*

SAY Moses was afraid to go. But God promised to be with Moses and teach Moses what to say to the people. God sent Moses' brother Aaron to help him. Now Moses was ready to trust God and obey his call. Moses was ready to serve God because he knew that God was with him and would help him!

☆Let's Make

Tear some strips of **tissue paper** in **orange, red,** and **yellow** colors. Help the children glue them to the bush. Wonder together how Moses felt when he heard God speak to him through the fire.

☆Let's Act

Tell the children that God tells us what he is like in the Bible. He is with us and gives us the help we need to trust and obey Jesus every day. Lead children in taking turns to act out one way they can listen to God's Word and serve Jesus. The rest of the group can guess what action is being pantomimed. Examples: praying, singing God's praises, sharing with others, listening carefully to God's Word, helping with chores, etc.

☆Let's Pray

Join hands in a circle. Have the children say each line of this prayer after you.

> Dear God, thank you for loving and calling me.
> Help me to trust and obey you.
> Help me to serve you each day.
> In Jesus' name, Amen.

Moses and Aaron spoke to Pharaoh.

Exodus 5–6

Moses and Aaron spoke to Pharaoh.
Exodus 5–6

☆Let's Talk and Wonder

ASK Look at the picture. *Why do you think Pharaoh, the king of Egypt, looks angry?*

SAY Moses and Aaron went to Pharaoh. Moses told the king to let the Israelites go so they could serve God. Pharaoh got angry. He would not let the Israelites go. He made them work even harder than before. They had to gather straw, make bricks, and build cities for the Egyptians.

ASK *What did the tired Israelites say to Moses and Aaron?*

SAY The Israelites told Moses and Aaron it was their fault. Moses felt terrible! He didn't know what to do next, so he prayed. God answered the prayer of Moses. God said he remembered his promises to Abraham and cared about his people's suffering. The Israelites were his own special people and he was their God. He would show his mighty power to everyone in Egypt and lead the Israelites out to the Promised Land. God wanted his people to trust him to save and help them!

SAY I wonder how the Israelites felt when Moses told them what God said . . .

☆Let's Make

❶ Tape a length of **butcher paper** to the table. Print **We Are God's People** across the top. Lead children in saying the caption as you point to the words. Remind them that God is always with his people, that he calls us to trust and obey him, and that he helps us.

❷ Hand out **crayons or markers.** Have the children draw God's people—themselves, families, pastor, Sunday school teacher, and friends. When they are finished, post the mural on the wall.

☆Let's Sing and Pray

Sing this prayer to the tune *Jesus Loves Me*. Sing each line and have children repeat after you.

> Thank you, God, for loving me,
> In your care I'll always be.
> Help me serve you every day,
> Show me what to do and say!

After singing, end the prayer by saying: **In Jesus' name, Amen.**

Exodus 5–6

© GCP www.gcp.org
OK to photocopy for church and home use

God sent 10 plagues on Egypt.
Exodus 7–10

God sent 10 plagues on Egypt.
Exodus 7–10

☆Let's Talk and Wonder

SAY Moses told Pharaoh to let the Israelites go so they could worship God. God wanted his people to worship him in their own land. But Pharaoh would not obey God's command. So God showed his mighty power and judgment by sending plagues to Egypt. First he changed the water of the Nile River into blood.

ASK *What did God do next? What do you see in the picture?*

SAY God sent frogs hopping all over the land. He sent 10 plagues in all. He made gnats and flies bother the Egyptians. The animals got sick and died. The Egyptians got sores. God sent a hailstorm that ruined their crops. A swarm of locusts came and ate all the plants and green leaves. God sent a deep darkness over Egypt. But Pharaoh still would not obey God!

SAY I wonder what it was like for the Israelites when God sent plagues to Egypt . . .

SAY God was getting ready to keep his promise to lead his people out of Egypt. Pharaoh could not stop God from keeping his promise. God is the Lord and he has power over everything! God was showing Pharaoh that the Israelites' God is the only true and living God.

☆Let's Whisper

Play *Telephone*. Sit in a circle. Whisper one of the sentences below to the child sitting next to you. That child whispers what he heard to the next child. Keep going until everyone has whispered and listened. The last child will then say what he heard out loud. Children will enjoy comparing the final message to the original message! Play again, starting with a different child.

God made rivers and frogs.
God made bugs and animals.
God made thunder, lightning, and hail!
God made locusts.
God made the wind.

God made light and darkness.
God made everything.
God has power over all he made.
We can trust our powerful God!

☆Let's Sing

Sing "My God Is So Big." Let the children add their own informal actions and move around the room as they sing.

 *Preschool Vol. 1* CD
Songbook, p. 7

God's people celebrated the first Passover.

Exodus 11–12

God's people celebrated the first Passover.
Exodus 11–12

☆Let's Talk

SAY It was time for the Israelites to leave Egypt. God told Moses that he would send a terrible plague on Pharaoh and his people. The Lord passed over the land of Egypt, and the oldest son in every Egyptian family died.

ASK What happened to the Israelites?

SAY God kept his people safe. Every Israelite family put the blood of a perfect lamb on the doorframe of their house. When the Lord passed over, he saw the blood and saved his people from death.

ASK What does the picture show?

SAY Each family quickly ate a special Passover meal and prepared to leave Egypt in a hurry. God told his people to celebrate this day every year so they would not forget how he freed them from slavery.

ASK What happened next?

SAY Pharaoh was finally ready to obey God's command. He called Moses and told him the Israelites could go. God's people hurried out of Egypt. God had kept his promise to save and protect them and lead them out to worship him. One day, he would send the promised Savior!

☆Let's Play and Sing

Everyone sit in a circle. Choose a player to walk around outside the circle, gently touching the head of each child as the group sings the following song to the tune *Here We Go Round the Mulberry Bush*. At the end of the song, the player names the child he is touching. That child becomes the new player, and the previous player takes her place in the circle. The game continues as before.

Preschool Vol. 2 CD

> Thank you, Lord, for saving us,
> Saving us, saving us.
>
> Thank you, Lord, for saving us,
> We belong to you!

☆Let's Paste and Praise

❶ Draw the outline of a cross on **paper**. Tell children that many years after the first Passover, God sent Jesus, the Lamb of God, to be our Savior! He died on the cross to save all God's people from their sins. Everyone who trusts in Jesus is forgiven of sin and saved from sin and death.

❷ Let children express praise to God for saving them as they take turns putting **heart stickers** on the cross.

© GCP www.gcp.org
OK to photocopy for church and home use

God parted the Red Sea.

Exodus 13–15

God parted the Red Sea.
Exodus 13–15

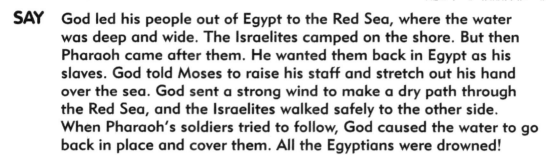

☆ Let's Talk

ASK *What do you see in the picture? What else?*

SAY God led his people out of Egypt to the Red Sea, where the water was deep and wide. The Israelites camped on the shore. But then Pharaoh came after them. He wanted them back in Egypt as his slaves. God told Moses to raise his staff and stretch out his hand over the sea. God sent a strong wind to make a dry path through the Red Sea, and the Israelites walked safely to the other side. When Pharaoh's soldiers tried to follow, God caused the water to go back in place and cover them. All the Egyptians were drowned!

ASK *What did the Israelites do when they saw how God saved, led, and protected them?*

SAY The Israelites were filled with joy and rejoiced in God their Savior. They sang his praises:
> The Lord is my strength and my song;
> He has become my salvation.
> He is my God, and I will praise him.

☆ Let's Pretend

Pretend to be Israelites following Moses on a journey from Egypt to the other side of the Red Sea. Have the children line up behind you as you give the following directions and wind your away around the room.

1. *Tiptoe* past Pharaoh.
2. *Crawl* past the Egyptians.
3. *Hop* over lizards in the desert.
4. *Go around* big rocks.
5. Set up camp by the Red Sea. *Lie down and go to sleep.*
6. *Walk slowly* across the Red Sea on dry ground.
7. You've made it to the other side. *Clap your hands and stomp your feet.*
8. You've left Egypt behind! *Sit down and rest.*

☆ Let's Sing and Play

Gather some **rhythm instruments** or use pot lids, wooden spoons, paper plate shakers filled with beans, and coffee can drums. Let children play their instruments as you lead them in singing this praise song to the tune *The Farmer in the Dell*.

The people praised the Lord,
He led them through the sea.
I will praise the Lord my God,
Because he cares for me!

track 45 Preschool Vol. 2 CD

God provided manna in the wilderness.
Exodus 16

God provided manna in the wilderness.
Exodus 16

☆ Let's Talk and Wonder

SAY As the Israelites traveled through the desert, they got hungry. The food they had brought from Egypt was gone. They grumbled that they were starving to death and blamed Moses and Aaron.

SAY I wonder if they forgot that God saved them from slavery. Or that he guided them with a cloud by day and fire by night. Or that he parted the Red Sea and made a dry path for them to walk across.

SAY Of course God would take care of his people! God would provide the food they needed.

ASK Look at the picture. *What are the Israelites doing?*

SAY In the morning the Israelites gathered bread, called manna, which God sent for them to eat. In the evening, God sent quail. People caught the birds and cooked them for supper. God gave his people the food they needed. The Israelites were learning that their powerful God could always be trusted to meet their needs!

☆ Let's Pretend and Paste

1. Cut **white paper** into small pieces. Draw the outline of a large basket on a **tan sheet of paper**.
2. Tell the children that while the Israelites were traveling to the Promised Land, they camped outdoors. Have everyone close their eyes and pretend to sleep. Quietly scatter the white pieces of paper on the floor. Then have the children open their eyes. Tell them that in the morning the Israelites saw white flakes covering the ground. God had sent food!
3. Let children collect the paper pieces and **glue** them in the basket one by one. Tell them that each family gathered just enough to eat that day. No more! When the basket is filled with "manna," remind children that we can trust Jesus to give us exactly what we need.

☆ Let's Snack and Pray

Snack on some **popcorn** (be aware of food allergies). Talk about God's care for us, and how he provides food and everything we need. Then teach them this simple prayer.

For giving us food to eat
Every single day,
For providing everything we need,
Thank you, Lord, we pray! In Jesus' name, Amen.

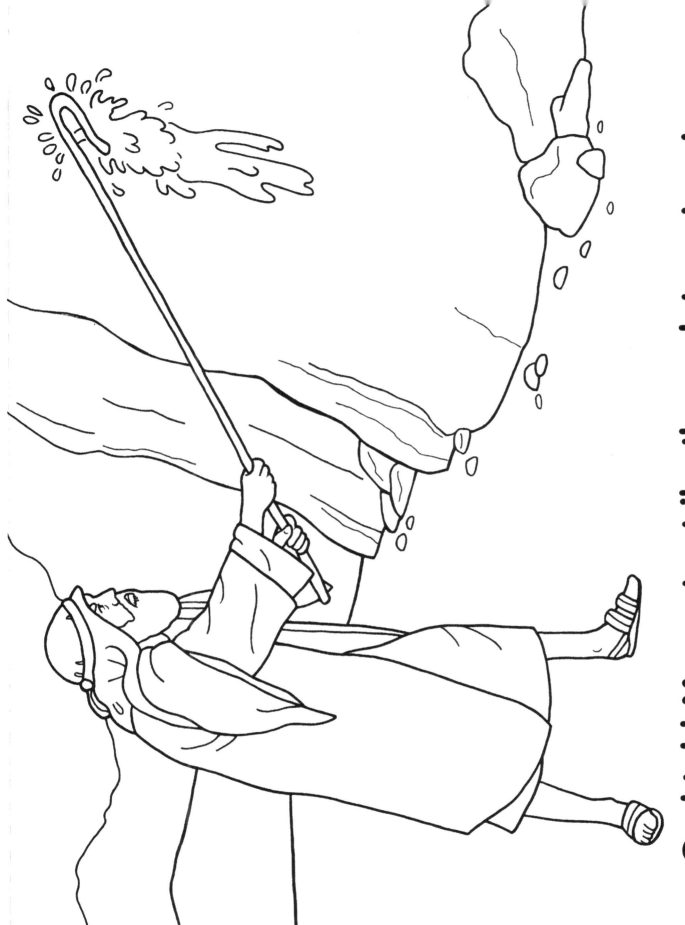

God told Moses to strike the rock to get water.
Exodus 17:1–7

☆Let's Talk

SAY God's people had walked all day in the hot desert sun. They were very thirsty. When they stopped to rest, they could not find any water to drink. They complained angrily to Moses. Moses prayed and asked God for help.

ASK *What do you see in the picture?*

SAY God told Moses to hit a special rock with his staff. Moses did as God said, and water came gushing out of the rock. Everyone had plenty of water to drink.

ASK *What did the Israelites learn about God?*

SAY The Israelites saw once again that God was keeping his promise to take care of them. They needed food and water. God provided food when they were hungry and water when they were thirsty. God was mercifully providing for their needs despite their grumbling. He was patiently teaching them to trust him.

☆Let's Make

Give each child a sheet of **paper** and a **gray crayon or marker**. Have them draw and color a big rock on their papers. Then provide each child with a **drinking straw**. Pour a small splotch of **blue paint** in the center of each rock. Show the children how to blow through their straws to let the water "flow" from the rock across the paper. Ask the children to picture what it must have been like when Moses struck the rock and water came pouring out! Then remind children of this truth: Jesus, our Savior, provides what we need.

☆Let's Rhyme

Teach your children the following rhyme. Emphasize the syllables that are capitalized.

❶ God **GIVES** me **ALL I NEED**,
EVery **SIN**gle **DAY**.
I **CAN** de**PEND** on **HIM**,
When **I'M** at **REST** or **PLAY**!

❷ I **THANK** God **FOR** his **CARE**,
For **WATCH**ing **O**ver **ME**.
I'll **TRUST** him **AND** o**BEY**—
His **CHILD** I'll **AL**ways **BE**!

God told Moses to hold up his arms to win the battle.

Exodus 17:8–16

God told Moses to hold up his arms to win the battle.
Exodus 17:8–16

☆Let's Talk

SAY God's people were traveling through the land of the Amalekites. The Amalekites started attacking the Israelites. Moses sent Joshua and a group of men to fight them off. Moses took Aaron and Hur to the top of a hill.

ASK Look at the picture. *What do you see?*

SAY Moses lifted the staff of God in his hands. As long as Moses held up his hands, God's people would win. When Moses put down his tired hands, the Israelites would start to lose. Moses sat down on a rock to rest and Aaron and Hur held up Moses' hands.

ASK *What do you think happened at the end of the day?*

SAY At sundown, Moses was able to put down his hands. God had caused the Israelites to win the battle. God told Moses to write everything down on a scroll so the people would remember what God had done that day. Moses did as God said, then he worshiped God. He thanked God for helping the Israelites win the battle.

☆Let's Do

Lead the children in the following action rhyme, doing the actions the words suggest. It will remind them of God's care for his people.

God gave me feet that can walk and run,
God gave me hands that reach to the sun.

God gave me legs that bend at the knees,
God gave me a nose that can twitch and sneeze.

God gave me food and somewhere to live,
God gave me a family with love to give.

So I thank God for all his great care,
He's good to his children everywhere!

☆Let's Show, Tell, and Pray

Tell children that the Bible is God's Word and that God's Word is true. The Bible tells us what God wants us to know. The story Moses wrote down is found in the Bible in Exodus. Pass your **Bible** around. Ask children to name other stories they've heard from God's Word. The Bible is about Jesus, who saves us from our sin.

Pray this prayer.

Dear God, thank you that your Word, the Bible, is true. Help us to trust in Jesus and your Word. Thank you for your promise to save, guide, and protect us. In Jesus' name, Amen.

Moses received God's Ten Commandments.

Exodus 19–20, 24

Moses received God's Ten Commandments.
Exodus 19–20, 24

☆ Let's Talk

SAY God led the Israelites to Mount Sinai. They camped in the desert at the foot of the mountain. God gave Moses a message for the people. God reminded them that he brought them out of Egypt and took care of them. God told them that they were to be faithful to him and obey him. They would always be God's special people. Then the mountain shook. Fire, smoke, thunder, and loud trumpet blasts came from the mountain!

ASK *What happened?*

SAY God was showing his great glory. He was getting ready to speak to his people from the mountain. God promised to be the Lord their God.

ASK Look at the picture. *What did God give Moses on the mountain?*

SAY God gave Moses tablets of stone. God had written the Ten Commandments on them. God had saved his people and told them how to please him!

☆ Let's Go

1 Write *desert* on a sheet of **yellow construction paper** and *Mount Sinai* on a **gray sheet**. Tape the signs on opposite walls. Have children gather in the center of the room.

2 Explain that when you call out a few words from the Bible story they must race to the sign where that part of the story took place. Then have them return to the center and wait for the words you say next. Continue this way to the end of the activity.

- **Moses told the people what God said.** *(desert)*
- **fire, smoke** *(Mount Sinai)*
- **thunder and trumpet blasts** *(Mount Sinai)*
- **The people camped.** *(desert)*
- **Moses received the tablets of stone.** *(Mount Sinai)*

☆ Let's Pray

Sit quietly and pray together.

> Dear God, thank you for your promise to be our God. You've given us your wonderful law. But just like the Israelites, we have sinful hearts and cannot obey perfectly. Thank you for sending Jesus to obey perfectly and to die for all our sins. Please forgive our sins and help us trust and obey you more. In Jesus' name, Amen.

Keep the Lord's Day holy.

Exodus 20:8

Keep the Lord's Day holy.
Exodus 20:8

☆Let's Talk

ASK *What do you see in the picture?*

SAY God saved his people from slavery and through Moses, God gave them the Ten Commandments so that they would know how to love God and love others. The fourth commandment teaches that God gave the Sabbath as a day set apart to rest and to worship God.

ASK *What day of the week is the Lord's Day?*

SAY The Lord's Day is Sunday, the Christian Sabbath. God tells his people to keep the Lord's Day holy by resting from the usual kind of work we do during the week. He wants us to enjoy him in a special way by worshiping him with his people, thinking about him, and doing kind and helpful things for others.

☆Let's Make

❶ Hand out **construction paper** and **crayons**. Let the children draw pictures of different ways they can keep the Lord's Day holy. They can draw pictures of themselves going to Sunday school, singing God's praises in church, listening to God's Word carefully, resting, visiting a friend who is sick, and so on.

❷ Cut out the pictures and **glue** them on a large sheet of **poster board** to make a collage. Print the words **We keep the Lord's Day holy** on it.

☆Let's Sing

Sing this song to the tune *Here We Go Round the Mulberry Bush*. Stand in a circle and dramatize the actions of each verse.

1. This is the way we *celebrate*,
   We *celebrate*, we *celebrate*,
   This the way we *celebrate*
   On the Lord's Day.

2. This is the way we *go to church* . . .
3. This is the way we *sing a hymn* . . .
4. This is the way we *hear God's Word* . . .
5. This is the way we *hug a friend* . . .
6. This is the way we *help someone* . . .
7. This is the way we *get some rest* . . .

Join hands and repeat the first verse as a finale!

Moses broke the tablets when he saw the golden calf idol.

Exodus 32–34

Moses broke the tablets when he saw the golden calf idol.

Exodus 32–34 (Exodus 20:4–6)

☆Let's Talk

SAY God's people said they would obey God's commandments. But while Moses was up on Mount Sinai, the people, led by Aaron, made a golden calf and worshiped it. When Moses came down and saw what the people were doing, he threw down the stones on which the Ten Commandments were written.

ASK *Why was Moses so upset?*

SAY The people had broken their promise to God. They disobeyed God when they made and worshiped an idol instead of God.

ASK *What did God do?*

SAY God did not destroy his people, as they deserved. He punished those who sinned against him and spared the rest. God forgave his people and continued to be their God, showing love to them and caring for their needs.

ASK *What do you think Moses did next?*

SAY Moses went back up Mount Sinai. The Lord gave Moses his commandments on two new stone tablets and Moses carried them down to the people.

☆Let's Sing and Do

Sing "Father, Lead Me Day by Day." Afterward, lead the children in saying these words and doing these actions.

Preschool Vol. 2 CD track 4 Songbook, p. 10

God loves me. *(place hands over heart)*
God leads me. *(point up)*
God teaches me. *(hold hands together to make a Bible)*
God shows me. *(fold hands in prayer)*
God forgives me. *(form a cross with two index fingers or with both arms)*

☆Let's Pray

Lead children in saying this prayer, phrase by phrase.

Dear God, thank you for loving me. Please forgive my sins. Give me a heart that wants to worship Jesus alone. Please help me to trust and obey you more and more. In Jesus' name, Amen.

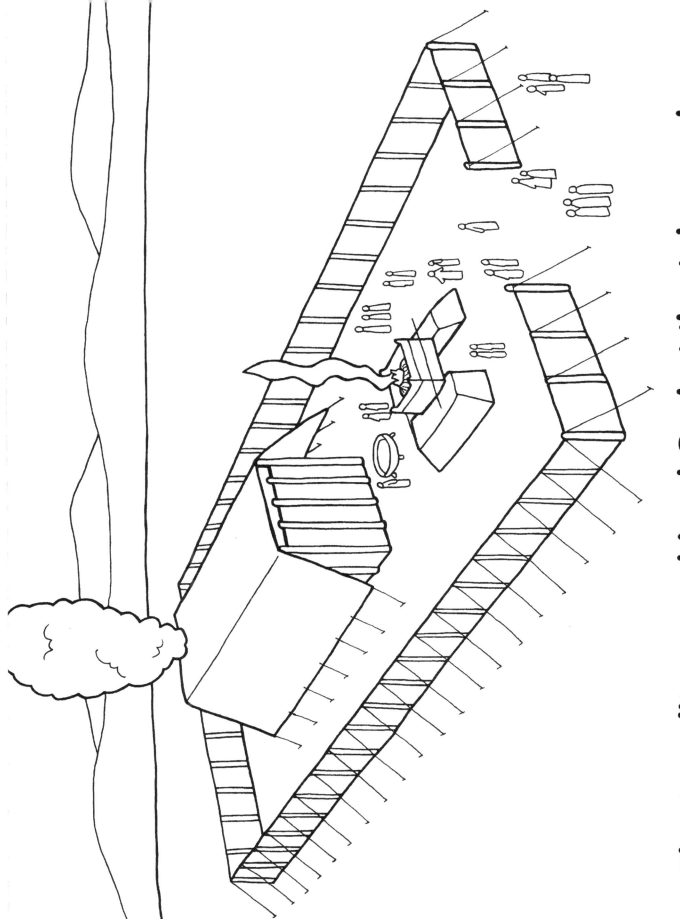

The Israelites worshiped God at the tabernacle.
Exodus 35–40

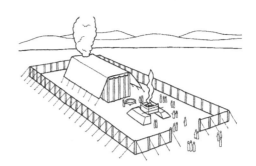

The Israelites worshiped God at the tabernacle.
Exodus 35–40

☆Let's Talk

SAY God told Moses to make a tabernacle, which was a tent for the Lord. God gave him a pattern showing exactly how it should be built.

ASK *Why did God tell the people to make a tent for him?*

SAY God would live there among his people and meet with them when they came to worship him. Moses told the people the details of God's plan, and they carefully made the tabernacle just as God commanded.

ASK Look at the picture. *What do you see?*

SAY The tabernacle itself was a large tent with two rooms. The larger room was called the Holy Place. The smaller room was the Most Holy Place, where the ark of the covenant was. Outside the tent was a courtyard surrounded by a fence made of curtains. In the courtyard were the altar of burnt offering and a basin where the priests washed their hands and feet before entering the tent.

SAY Every time a person went to the tabernacle to worship God, he had to take a lamb to be sacrificed for his sins. God's people looked forward to the day when the Savior would come. When Jesus came, he took the punishment for all the sins of all God's people when he died on the cross. We don't sacrifice animals to pay the price for our sins. We come to God by trusting in Jesus, our Savior!

☆Let's Do

Draw the outline of a cross on a large sheet of **construction paper**. Across the top, write in block letters: *I can come to God through trusting Jesus, my Savior.* Let children color the cross and the letters. Talk about how glad we are that God planned a way for his children to come to him. We can thank God for sending the promised Savior!

☆Let's Sing

Lead the children in singing this simple song to the tune *The Farmer in the Dell*.

We can come to God,
We can come to God.
We can come to God today
Through Jesus Christ, our Lord!

The spies brought grapes from the Promised Land.

Numbers 13–14

 **The spies brought grapes from the Promised Land.**
Numbers 13–14

☆Let's Talk and Wonder

SAY God led his people to the edge of Canaan. Moses sent 12 spies to explore the land God promised to give them. When they came back, they reported on the land.

ASK Look at the picture. *What are the men carrying?*

SAY The men saw that the Promised Land was good for growing food. They brought back a cluster of grapes to show everyone how fruitful the land was.

ASK *Did all the spies think that the Israelites could conquer the people living in the land?*

SAY Most of the spies thought the people in the land were too strong and that Israel wouldn't be able to win the battle for the land. But two spies, Joshua and Caleb, said the Israelites should go in and take the land. They trusted that God would do what he said, be with them, and give them victory in the land.

☆Let's Sing and Pretend

Lead the children in doing these actions as they sing about the journey to the tune *Here We Go Round the Mulberry Bush*.

This is the way we go to Canaan, *(walk around the room)*
Go to Canaan, go to Canaan.
This is the way we go to Canaan,
So early in the morning.

Include these verses:

- **This is the way we explore the land** *(look around, shade eyes with hand)*
- **This is the way we gather fruit** *(pretend to pick clusters of grapes from vines)*
- **This is the way we return with the news** *(crowd around in the center of the room)*
- **This is the way we conquer the land** *(point up, then fold hands in prayer)*

☆Let's Name Ways

God wants us to trust Jesus, his Son. Ask children to name one way they can show they trust Jesus. They can ask for his help, trust his promises, and obey his commands. Remind them that Jesus is always with them and that he is always faithful!

Moses and Aaron led the Israelites, who often rebelled.

Numbers 16–17

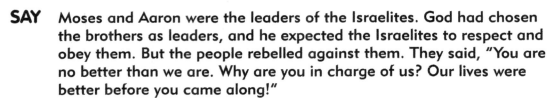

Moses and Aaron led the Israelites, who often rebelled.
Numbers 16–17

☆Let's Talk

ASK *Who do you see in the picture?*

SAY Moses and Aaron were the leaders of the Israelites. God had chosen the brothers as leaders, and he expected the Israelites to respect and obey them. But the people rebelled against them. They said, "You are no better than we are. Why are you in charge of us? Our lives were better before you came along!"

ASK *Was God happy that the people did not trust his leaders?*

SAY God punished the people who disobeyed. The ground opened up and swallowed some, and fire destroyed others.

ASK *Did the people stop complaining about Moses and Aaron?*

SAY The next day, they grumbled again and God punished those who complained. Moses told Aaron to make an offering to the Lord for the sins of the people. Then God showed the Israelites that he didn't want to destroy them. The people were sorry for their sin. Each time they came to the tabernacle to worship God, they remembered that they must honor and obey those whom God had chosen to lead them. When people complain against God's leaders, God says they are complaining against him.

☆Let's Make

Print *People Who Are in Charge of Us* across the top of a large sheet of **poster board**. Hand out **old children's magazines, scissors,** and **glue**. Let children look through the magazines and cut out pictures they find of people who have authority over them (parent, pastor, teacher, coach, firefighter, etc.). Paste pictures on the poster board to make a collage. Display the finished collage. Let children talk about the pictures and discuss what God says it means to obey the leaders he puts in charge in our homes, our church, and our community.

☆Let's Pray

Ask the children to repeat each sentence of this prayer after you.

> Dear God, thank you for providing leaders to take care of me. Thank you for my parents, my pastor, and my teachers. Please help me to respect and obey them. In Jesus' name, Amen.

Moses lifted the bronze snake. Those who looked at it were healed.
Numbers 21:4–9

Moses lifted the bronze snake. Those who looked at it were healed.
Numbers 21:4–9

☆Let's Talk

SAY The Israelites grumbled a lot. They said they were tired of wandering around in the desert. They were sick of eating manna and they were always thirsty.

ASK *What had they forgotten?*

SAY The Israelites had forgotten God's promises and his goodness to them. Hadn't he provided for their needs, fought off their enemies, led them each day, and protected them from sickness and danger? Hadn't he promised to take care of them? They had not learned to trust God.

SAY God disciplined the Israelites by sending poisonous snakes into their camp. People were bitten and many died. The Israelites were sorry for their sin and asked Moses to pray that the Lord would take the snakes away and heal them.

ASK Look at the picture. *What do you see?*

SAY God left the snakes in the camp. But he told Moses to make a bronze snake and put it on a pole. God promised that everyone who looked at the bronze snake would be made well. Moses did as God said. All those who believed and looked up at the snake were healed. Many years later, Jesus was lifted up on the cross to die for our sins. Those who look to Jesus and trust in him are saved.

☆Let's Sing

Sing "My Help Comes from the Lord."
(to the tune Go, Tell It on the Mountain)

Younger Elementary Vol. 1 CD track 15
Songbook, p. 24

Chorus Go, tell it on the mountain, over the hills and everywhere;
Go, tell it on the mountain—My help comes from the Lord.

Verse 1 The King of all Creation; the one true God is he.
He is my great protector, because he cares for me.

Verse 2 He will not let me stumble; he will not let me fall.
The Lord himself is with me, and hears me when I call.

Verse 3 He watches over Israel, and never turns away.
He leads them step by step, and guards them night and day.

Verse 4 The Lord will keep his people; we're always in his care.
Our coming and our going; we have no need to fear.

Numbers 21

© GCP www.gcp.org
OK to photocopy for church and home use

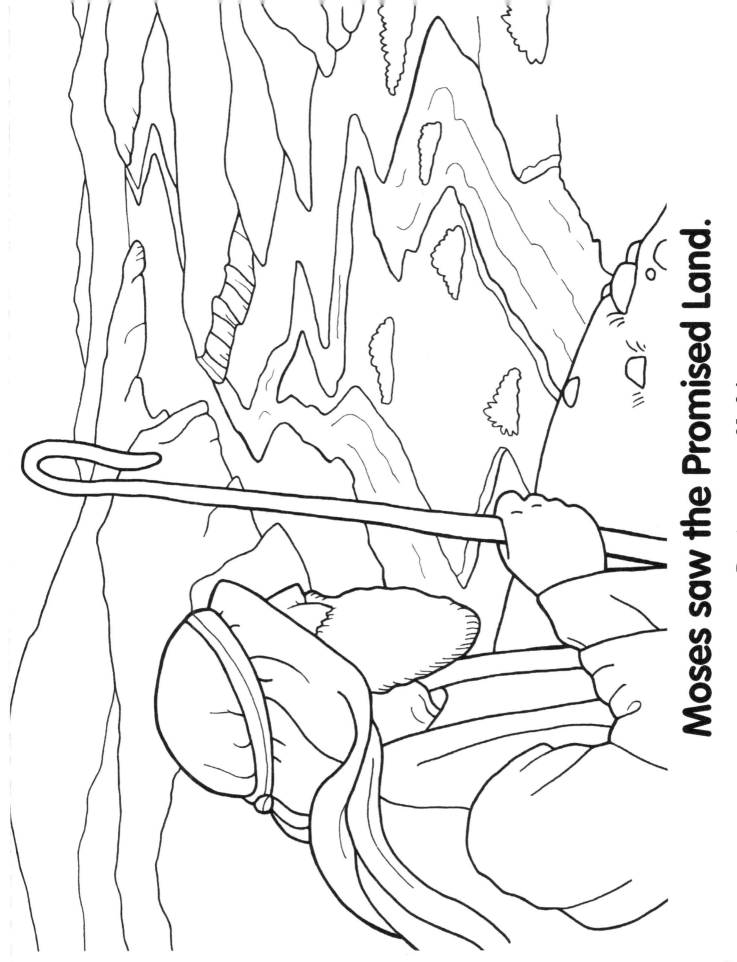

Moses saw the Promised Land.
Deuteronomy 31–34

☆Let's Talk and Wonder

SAY Moses was now an old man. He called the Israelites together and told them that Joshua would lead them into the new land. Moses reminded them that God loved them and would be with them, as he had promised. God had kept his Word to his people. God had brought them out of Egypt and taken care of them so they could worship him in Canaan, the Promised Land.

ASK Look at the picture. *What did Moses do next?*

SAY He climbed to the top of Mount Nebo. God showed him Canaan, and Moses was glad to see the beautiful Promised Land. His heart was filled with praise to the Lord. Then Moses died and God took Moses to live with him in heaven.

ASK God had made another important promise to his people. He had promised to send a Savior one day. *Did God keep his promise?*

SAY Many years later, God sent his Son, Jesus, to be the Savior. Jesus was born as a little baby in that very same land called Canaan. Later, he died on the cross for the sins of all God's people. Then he rose from the dead on the third day to live forever. Jesus is our living Savior!

☆Let's Make

When children have finished coloring, let them make touch-and-feel pictures. Provide one or more of the following items for children to **glue** onto their pictures: **green fabric, blue felt, rice, beans, glitter glue.**

☆Let's Show and Tell

❶ Show children a **picture of the cross**. Talk about how glad we are that God kept his promise to send the promised Savior. Remind them that Jesus, our Savior, is alive right now. His Spirit is with all those who believe in him as the Savior. Even though we cannot see him, Jesus hears us when we pray and helps us trust and obey him.

❷ Let children name one thing they can praise God for. Be sure to mention that we can praise him for loving us, for keeping his promises, for providing for our needs, and for sending Jesus to be our Savior.

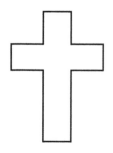

God parted the Jordan River so the people could cross.

Joshua 3–4

 **God parted the Jordan River so the people could cross.**
Joshua 3–4

☆Let's Talk

SAY After Moses died, God chose Joshua to lead the people of Israel. Joshua told them to roll up their tents and get ready to march into the Promised Land. The people obeyed. When they saw the priests walking toward the Jordan River carrying the ark of the covenant, they remembered that God was leading them.

ASK What do you see in the picture?

SAY When the priests reached the Jordan River, God piled the water up in a heap so that the riverbed was dry. Then the priests walked into the middle of the riverbed and stood there while all the Israelites crossed over into Canaan on dry land.

ASK What do you think happened next?

SAY Joshua told the priests to come out of the Jordan. As soon as they stepped out, the waters of the river roared down and started flowing again. Then Joshua used 12 stones from the river to build a monument. It was to remind them of God's goodness. God had kept his promises. He had taken care of his people and brought them safely to their new land!

☆Let's Eat and Share

Bring **fish crackers** and **blue punch or blue gelatin blocks** and **water**. (Be aware of food allergies.) Gather around the table to share the food. Have the children help pass out **napkins** and **cups**. As you snack, talk about what God did at the Jordan River. Ask children if they remember the time when God pushed the water back at the Red Sea and made a dry path for the Israelites. Talk about other times God protected his people and kept his promises to them—especially when Jesus came to die for his people's sin.

☆Let's Say and Pray

Invite the children to name ways God keeps his promises to us. Then say this prayer together.

> Dear God, thank you that you always keep your promises. Thank you for saving us and taking care of us. Help us trust and obey you. In Jesus' name, Amen.

God gave the Israelites victory at Jericho.
Joshua 6

 **God gave the Israelites victory at Jericho.**
Joshua 6

☆Let's Talk and Wonder

SAY Joshua was the new leader of God's people, the Israelites. Under Joshua, God brought his people into the Promised Land. The first city they came to was Jericho. Big stone walls surrounded the city. The people who lived inside were God's enemies and under his judgment. The Lord told Joshua that he would give Jericho to the Israelites. He told Joshua what to do, and then Joshua told the people God's plan.

SAY I wonder if the people did what God said . . .

SAY The Israelites carried out God's plan. Soldiers marched around the city walls one time each day for six days, and the priests carried trumpets and blew them. On the seventh day, they marched around the city walls seven times, with the priests blowing trumpets. When they blew their trumpets long and loud, all the people gave a loud shout and the walls tumbled to the ground.

SAY I wonder what the soldiers did when the walls of Jericho tumbled down . . .

SAY The soldiers ran inside and took the city! God gave his people Jericho by making the walls fall down. The city and God's enemies were destroyed! God's plan and God's promise was carried out.

☆Let's Act

Let the children pretend to be soldiers and priests. Form a line and parade around the room, as though marching around the walled city of Jericho. The soldiers can pretend to carry swords, and the priests can pretend to hold up their trumpets. As they march around the walls, priests can make trumpet sounds, while soldiers march silently, swords raised!

☆Let's Sing and Pray

Sing "My God Is So Big." Then gather in a circle for prayer. Ask children to repeat this prayer after you, sentence by sentence.

 Toddler Sing-Along With Me CD
Songbook, p. 29

> Dear God, you are great and powerful. Thank you that you take care of your people. Help us depend on you each day. In Jesus' name, Amen.

Joshua 6

© GCP www.gcp.org
OK to photocopy for church and home use

God made the sun stand still while Joshua led the battle.

Joshua 10

God made the sun stand still while Joshua led the battle.
Joshua 10

☆Let's Talk

SAY When God chose Joshua to be leader of the Israelites, God said three very important things. God told Joshua to be strong and courageous, God promised to be with him, and God told him to treasure God's laws and obey them.

ASK *What kind of leader was Joshua?*

SAY Joshua could be strong and courageous because he trusted in God. He trusted God to help him cross the Jordan River, lead the Israelites into the Promised Land, win the battle of Jericho, and win the battle at Gibeon.

ASK *What took place at Gibeon?*

SAY Enemy soldiers had gathered to fight against the Gibeonites. Israel had promised to fight with the Gibeonites. So Joshua and his men attacked at night. God sent hailstones that killed the enemy as they ran away. Then Joshua prayed that the sun and moon would stand still to make the day longer so they could finish the battle against their enemies.

ASK *What happened next?*

SAY God answered Joshua's prayer and Israel won the victory! Joshua and the Israelite army knew that God had fought and won the battle for them.

☆Let's Sing

Listen to "Be Strong" while the children color. The words of the song are about always trusting in Jesus. Then teach them the song. While children sing, have them march around the room and do motions suggested by the words.

Younger Elementary Vol. 2 CD
Songbook, p. 23

(track 10)

☆Let's Pray

Lead children in saying this prayer.

> Dear Lord, thank you that you are with me at all times. Help me to trust you and obey your Word. Please give me strength and courage to serve you today. In Jesus' name, Amen.

God gave Gideon a sign.
Judges 6–7

☆ Let's Talk

SAY The Israelites living in the Promised Land didn't teach their children to love and trust God. When the children became grown-ups, they disobeyed God and worshiped idols. God punished them by sending an enemy, the Midianites, into their land to rob them. The frightened Israelites turned back to God and asked him to save them.

ASK *What do you think God did?*

SAY God heard their cries for help. He chose Gideon, a farmer, to lead the Israelites in driving the Midianites out of their land. Gideon asked God for a sign.

ASK *What do you see in the picture?*

SAY God gave Gideon a sign. An angel told Gideon to put food he had prepared on a rock. The angel touched the food, and flames burst from the rock and burned up the food. Then God gave him another sign. Gideon was sure God wanted him to lead Israel against the Midianites.

SAY God used only 300 men to attack the Midianites, who had a huge army. The Israelites surprised them at night. The Midianites were so badly beaten they ran off and never dared come back. The Israelites knew that their little army hadn't won the battle. God had won it for them. As long as Gideon was alive, the Israelites worshiped God. They remembered all that God had done for them and how much they needed him!

☆ Let's Draw

Tape a length of **butcher paper** to the table. Have the children draw pictures that show something God does for them. Remind the children that we must depend on Jesus because he gives us what we need.

☆ Let's Listen and Sing

Listen to and sing "Trusting in the Lord." *Younger Elementary Vol. 1* CD
Songbook, p. 25

Samson trusted God to give him strength.

Judges 13–16

Samson trusted God to give him strength.
Judges 13–16

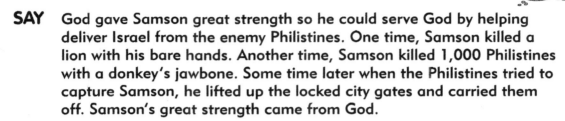

☆Let's Talk and Wonder

SAY God gave Samson great strength so he could serve God by helping deliver Israel from the enemy Philistines. One time, Samson killed a lion with his bare hands. Another time, Samson killed 1,000 Philistines with a donkey's jawbone. Some time later when the Philistines tried to capture Samson, he lifted up the locked city gates and carried them off. Samson's great strength came from God.

ASK *Did Samson always remember to serve God?*

SAY Samson did not always serve God. He disobeyed God's law over and over. Eventually the Philistines captured Samson. They blinded him, threw him into prison, and made him work hard grinding grain.

SAY I wonder how Samson felt when that happened . . .

SAY After a while, the Philistines held a great festival in honor of their false god. They led Samson into the crowded enemy temple and made fun of him. Samson prayed to God, asking for strength one more time. He then pushed hard against the pillars, and the temple crashed down, killing everyone, even Samson. In the end, Samson remembered that his strength came from God, and he trusted God to deliver Israel from their enemies, the Philistines.

God sent Jesus to deliver us from our enemy—our sin and the devil. Jesus never sinned. Because he is God, he defeated the devil when he died on the cross for our sin.

☆Let's Draw

Hand out **paper** and **crayons or markers**. Have the children draw some things mentioned in this story (for example, a lion, a donkey, city gates, the temple, Samson). Have children tell about Samson as they show their pictures.

☆Let's Pray

Lead the children in saying sentence prayers asking God to help them trust and obey him.

Ruth and Naomi trusted God.

Ruth 1–4

Ruth and Naomi trusted God.
Ruth 1–4

☆Let's Talk

SAY Ruth, whose husband had died, was ready to go back to Bethlehem with Naomi, her mother-in-law. "Where you go I will go," Ruth said. "Your people will be my people and your God my God." Ruth loved Naomi, who was alone and sad because her husband and sons had died. Ruth wanted to be with Naomi because Ruth trusted in the God of Israel and wanted to serve him.

ASK What happened when Ruth and Naomi got to Bethlehem?

SAY The two women were poor and had little food. So Ruth went to the field to pick up the barley that was left behind as the grain was being harvested. She worked hard all day, and the owner of the field, Boaz, who was related to Naomi, took notice. He was pleased that Ruth was loyal and kind to Naomi.

ASK What did Naomi say when Ruth told her that she had worked all day in the field belonging to Boaz?

SAY Naomi told her to go back to Boaz and ask for his protection. Naomi hoped that Boaz would take care of her and Ruth. Boaz agreed to take care of Naomi. Then Boaz married Ruth. God provided everything Ruth and Naomi needed.

ASK What happened after Ruth and Boaz got married?

SAY They had a baby boy named Obed. He became the grandfather of King David. Many years later, Jesus was born in Bethlehem. God sent his Son, Jesus, to be the Savior from the family line of Naomi, Ruth, Boaz, Obed, and David!

☆Let's Share and Show

❶ Talk about Ruth's friendship with Naomi. Then suggest ways that God might use the children to show Jesus' love to others. Children may share examples from their own experience—people they have helped, or who may have helped them with a smile, a hug, a kind word, and so on.

❷ Make **cards** or **drawings** for someone who needs Jesus or cheer and encouragement. Pray for that person, then let children make cards and drawings to send to him or her. Ask them to dictate a message about Jesus for you to write on each drawing or card. Have them sign their cards. Collect the finished cards, put them in a large **envelope,** and send them to the person you've selected.

Hannah praised God for giving her a son, Samuel.
1 Samuel 1–2

Hannah praised God for giving her a son, Samuel.
1 Samuel 1–2

☆Let's Talk

SAY Hannah was sad. She wanted a baby more than anything. Hannah and her husband went to the tabernacle, the place where people worshiped God. She prayed, "Dear God, please give me a son. I will give him to you to serve you all the days of his life." Eli, the priest, saw Hannah praying. "Go home with a peaceful heart," he told her. "The Lord has heard your prayer."

ASK *How do you think Hannah felt when she left the tabernacle?*

SAY When Hannah and her husband went home, she wasn't sad anymore. After some time, she and her husband had a baby boy named Samuel. Hannah praised and thanked God for his wonderful gift.

ASK *What do you think Hannah said in her prayer?*

SAY Hannah said the Lord had filled her heart with joy. She rejoiced in the Lord and was glad that he had helped her. Hannah said that no one is holy like God. He is the only true God. The earth belongs to him and he knows everything!

ASK *What did Hannah do with young Samuel?*

SAY Hannah took him to live at the tabernacle with Eli, the priest. Samuel served the Lord in a special way his whole life, just as Hannah prayed he would.

☆Let's Thank and Praise

1. Ahead of time, cut out **pictures from magazines** of things children can thank God for (a baby brother or sister, home, food, pet, friends, etc.). Put the pictures in a **bag**.

2. Show the children the bag. Explain that it contains things we'll thank our wonderful God for. Give each child an opportunity to pull out a picture and show it to everyone. When everyone sees the picture, lead the group in saying, **"Thank you, God, for . . .** *(name the thing shown in the picture).***"** Continue until all the pictures have been pulled from the bag.

3. Conclude this activity by saying: **"We praise God for his goodness to us! We thank him for the wonderful gifts he gives us, especially the gift of Jesus!"**

Samuel heard God calling his name.

1 Samuel 3

Samuel heard God calling his name.
1 Samuel 3

☆Let's Talk

SAY When Samuel was a young boy, his mother, Hannah, took him to live with Eli the priest so he could love and serve God in the house of the Lord. One night, Samuel was lying in bed when he heard someone call his name.

ASK *What happened when Samuel heard his name called?*

SAY Samuel got up and ran to Eli, but the old priest had not called him. It was the Lord who was calling Samuel! Eli told Samuel to listen for God's voice. Again God called his name. Samuel answered, "Speak, Lord, for your servant is listening." Samuel listened carefully as God spoke to him. God had chosen Samuel to belong to him and serve him. The next morning, he told Eli everything the Lord said.

ASK *Did Samuel obey God's call?*

SAY Samuel obeyed God's call. He served God because God was with him and gave him the power to do so. When he grew up, Samuel began to lead God's people back to the Lord and his Word.

☆Let's Listen and Obey

Play *The Bible Says*, which is like *Simon Says*. The children may do the actions below only if you say *"The Bible says . . ."* before each command.

- *The Bible says* God keeps his promises. High-five your friend next to you.
- Hop on one foot.
- Wiggle your fingers. Now pat your head.
- *The Bible says* God watches over you. Reach up high and turn around.
- *The Bible says* God calls you to serve him. Open your hands, palms facing up.
- Cover your ears with your hands.
- *The Bible says* trust and obey Jesus. Open your hands as a book.

☆Let's Whisper a Prayer

Invite everyone to whisper this prayer together.

> Dear God, help me grow in trusting and obeying you.
> In Jesus' name, Amen.

 **Hophni and Phinehas did not honor God or obey their father.**

1 Samuel 2:12–4:18 (Exodus 20:12)

☆Let's Talk

SAY Eli, the high priest, had two sons, Hophni and Phinehas. They served as priests at the tabernacle, but they did not obey God's law. Some of the people told Eli that his sons were leading the people to sin against God!

ASK Look at the picture. *What do you think Eli did?*

SAY Eli told his sons that he had heard they were doing terrible things. He warned them about sinning against God. But Hophni and Phinehas paid no attention to their father's warning. They went right on doing as they pleased.

SAY Eli did not punish his sons. God sent a prophet to warn Eli of coming judgment on his family. God punished Eli and his sons because they did not put God first and obey his Word. Hophni and Phinehas did not honor their father either.

SAY God tells us in the fifth commandment to honor our parents.

☆Let's Do

Have everyone sit on the floor. Tell the children that you if you say something that shows obedience, they must cross their hands over their heart. If you say something that shows disobedience, they should give a thumbs-down sign and shake their heads sadly.

Shows obedience
- Learn and obey God's Word
- Pray
- Obey mom or dad
- Listen when the pastor preaches
- Be kind and loving

Shows disobedience
- Be mean
- Push and shove
- Disobey God's Word
- Take things that are not mine
- Don't listen to mom or dad

Remind the children that when we disobey, we can say we were wrong and ask Jesus to forgive us.

☆Let's Sing and Pray

Sing this prayer line by line to the tune *Jesus Loves Me*.

Verse Thank you, Lord, for loving me,
And for teaching me your ways.
Help me trust you and obey,
By your Word, guide all my days.

Chorus I'll follow Jesus
I'll follow Jesus,
I'll follow Jesus,
The Bible tells me how!

track 39 *Preschool Vol. 1 CD*

1 Samuel 2–4

 **Samuel told King Saul he disobeyed God.**
1 Samuel 13

☆Let's Talk

SAY The people of Israel complained that Samuel was too old to be their prophet. They wanted a king. Samuel prayed, and God told him to give them a king. But God said to warn the people that having the kind of king they wanted would make their lives harder, not easier.

ASK *Who was chosen as king?*

SAY God chose Saul to lead the people. At first, Saul did a good job. He won his first battle and praised God for it. He listened to Samuel's advice and told the people to do the same. But then everything changed.

ASK *What do you think happened?*

SAY When the powerful Philistines got ready to attack Israel, Saul disobeyed God's command. Instead of waiting for the prophet Samuel to make the sacrifice to the Lord before going into battle, Saul did it himself when he saw his soldiers running away.

ASK *What do you see in the picture?*

SAY Samuel was very disappointed at what Saul did. "You acted foolishly," he told Saul. "If you had trusted and obeyed God, you would have continued to be king of Israel. But now you have lost the kingdom God gave you!"

☆Let's Make and Discuss

SAY Even though Saul didn't obey God perfectly, Jesus did! Jesus did everything God told him to do. He died on the cross so that we who disobey can be forgiven. Now Jesus is our risen King! He leads us and helps us obey and do the right thing even when it is hard.

1. Cut out **brown paper** wooden beams to make a cross. Let the children **glue** the cross on a large sheet of **construction paper**.
2. Put out **fingerpaint**. Have the children make a border with their fingertips. Don't forget **cleanup supplies**!

As they work, ask the children to mention a time when it was hard for them to obey Jesus. Remind them that when they disobey, they can ask Jesus for forgiveness and pray for his help to trust and obey him.

Samuel anointed David as king.
1 Samuel 16:1–13

☆Let's Talk

ASK *Why did Samuel send for David the shepherd boy, the son of Jesse?*

SAY God told Samuel to anoint David because one day David would become king of Israel. So Samuel took a horn of oil and poured it on David's head in front of his family. From that day on God's Spirit was with David.

ASK *What did David do next?*

SAY David went back to being a shepherd because it was not yet time to serve as king. His heart was filled with trust in the Lord. He knew that God would give him the strength and help he needed to be a good king when the time came.

ASK *Who is our perfect King?*

SAY God provided a perfect Savior-King for us. Many years after David was king, God sent Jesus, born from David's family, to die for our sins. God's Son, Jesus, is our perfect Lord and King. He rules over us and he defends us!

☆Let's Touch and Feel

1. Bring to class a **stuffed sheep toy** and a **toy crown**. First, invite everyone to look at and touch the soft sheep. Talk with the children about David's job as a shepherd, and how he needed to protect, feed, and guide the sheep.

2. Then have everyone look at the crown and feel it. Talk about the job of a king. A good king protects, takes care of, and guides those who are ruled by him.

3. Explain that Jesus is our perfect Shepherd and King. He protects, feeds, and guides those who are in his care every day!

☆Let's Sing

Listen to and sing "We Thank Thee, Loving Father." Join hands and sing together this additional verse:

Preschool Vol. 1 CD (track 21)
Songbook, p. 28

> We thank Thee, loving Father,
> That Jesus is our King,
> Our Ruler and Defender—
> His praises we will sing!

1 Samuel 16

© GCP www.gcp.org
OK to photocopy for church and home use

David, the shepherd boy, sang songs of praise to God.

1 Samuel 16

David, the shepherd boy, sang songs of praise to God.
1 Samuel 16

☆ Let's Talk

SAY When David was young, he took care of his father's sheep.

ASK *What did David need to do to care for the sheep?*

SAY He took the sheep to find grass to eat and water to drink. He made sure they didn't wander off and he protected them from danger. David was a brave shepherd. He even killed a bear and a lion when they came after the sheep.

ASK Look at the picture. *What else did David do?*

SAY David played his harp and sang songs of praise to God. These songs are called psalms and are in our Bible. David trusted in our loving God. The young shepherd knew that it was God who protected him from all kinds of danger and gave him strength. David thanked God in Psalm 18:1 by singing, "I love you, O Lord, my strength."

☆ Let's Make, Play, and Praise

❶ Make simple musical instruments.

Maracas: Fill empty soda bottles a third full of sand or small pebbles; shake.

Chimes: Hang metal washers or key rings on strings from a ruler; strike the washers with a spoon.

Harp or guitar: Put rubber bands around an empty shoebox; strum the "strings."

Cymbals: Strike pot lids together.

❷ Play the instruments as you sing together the words of praise David wrote in Psalm 18. Sing to the tune *Away in a Manger*.

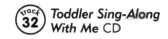

Toddler Sing-Along With Me CD

> I love you, O Lord, I love you, Lord.
> I love you, Lord, for you are my strength.
> I love you, O Lord, I love you, Lord,
> I love you, Lord, for you are my strength.

☆ Let's Pray

Lead children in this prayer.

Dear God, thank you for loving us and taking care of us. We want to tell you some more things we're thankful for. *(Let children take turns naming things or people they are thankful for.)* **We praise you for being so good. In Jesus' name, Amen.**

1 Samuel 16

© GCP www.gcp.org
OK to photocopy for church and home use

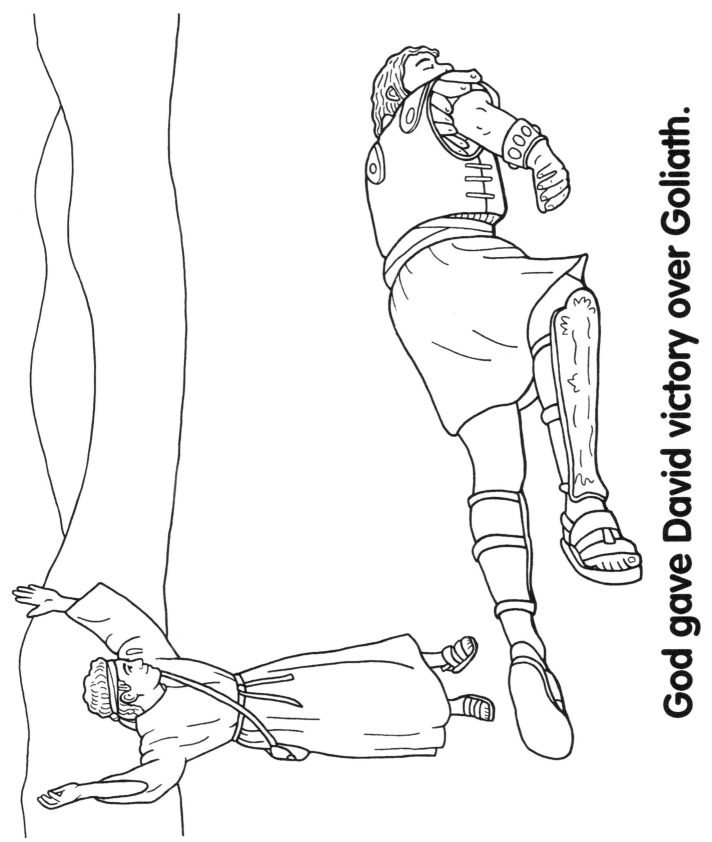

 **God gave David victory over Goliath.**
1 Samuel 17

☆Let's Talk

ASK *What do you see in the picture?*

SAY God did something very special through David. God called David and used him to deliver his people from Goliath and the Philistines. David was much smaller than Goliath and all he had to fight with were a shepherd's staff, a bag with five stones, and a sling. When the warrior Goliath saw the shepherd boy, he laughed.

ASK *What did David tell Goliath just before he killed him?*

SAY David said to the champion soldier, "You have a sword and a spear with you, but I have the Lord God with me. I come against you in his all-powerful name. The battle is the Lord's and he will win."

ASK *Why did David trust God?*

SAY David knew that God had called him and was with him. He had protected David before, and he would give David all he needed to deliver God's people from their enemy. Also, David knew that God had promised to be faithful to his people. God had promised to send Jesus the Savior one day.

☆Let's Make and Remember

Using **play dough,** have the children make figures representing David and Goliath. They can also make David's stones and Goliath's sword.

Encourage everyone to use the props to retell the Bible story of David and Goliath.

☆Let's Draw and Say

❶ Talk about times when we have faced something big and scary and how we can always trust God to help us. Point out that God is more powerful than all things that trouble us.

❷ Hand out **paper** and **crayons or markers**. Draw self-portraits. Write on each picture: *I can trust God to help me in times of trouble.* Help children write their names on their papers.

❸ Invite children to hold up their self-portraits for everyone to see. As they do, say the caption together.

King Saul was jealous of David.
1 Samuel 18 (Exodus 20:17)

☆Let's Talk

ASK *What do you see in the picture?*

SAY When David was young, he played his harp for King Saul. The king enjoyed it. At first, the king was very pleased with David. But after a while the king became jealous of the gifted young man.

ASK *Why did Saul become jealous of David?*

SAY God's Spirit was with David as a young shepherd. David trusted in the power of the Lord. God gave David victory over Goliath, the enemy of Israel. When Saul made David a commander in the army, the young man became a great leader and all the people praised him. God chose David to be the next king after Saul. So, Saul grew angry and jealous as David became more popular. Saul wanted keep being king. Saul coveted what God had given David.

SAY After Saul died, David was crowned king. And many, many years later, our Savior, Jesus, was born from David's family!

☆Let's Play

Before playing the following game, talk about coveting. Point out that it means being jealous of what others have and not being content. Remind children that the tenth commandment, Exodus 20:17, says to not covet. *Say* **God provides for the needs of his children. We can be content—that is, thankful and satisfied—because everything we have comes from him.**

Stand in a circle to play *Be Content Ball Toss*. Toss the **ball** to someone in the circle and ask her to name something she is thankful to God for. Then have the child toss the ball back to you. Continue playing until everyone has had a turn.

Let's Sing

Sing this prayer to the tune *Mary Had a Little Lamb*.

❶ Jesus, our Savior,
Our Savior, our Savior,
Jesus, our Savior,
Please forgive our sin.

❷ Help us to be thankful,
Be thankful, be thankful,
Help us to be thankful,
For all you've given us.

 *Preschool Vol. 2* CD

1 Samuel 18

© GCP www.gcp.org
OK to photocopy for church and home use

King Saul tried to kill David, but later he blessed him.

1 Samuel 26

King Saul tried to kill David, but later he blessed him.
1 Samuel 26

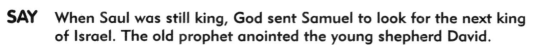

☆Let's Talk

SAY When Saul was still king, God sent Samuel to look for the next king of Israel. The old prophet anointed the young shepherd David.

ASK *What did Saul think of young David?*

SAY At first, Saul liked the young shepherd, who sometimes played the harp for the troubled king. David did everything well and was popular among the Israelites. But after a while, Saul became angry and jealous. He knew that one day the kingdom would be taken away from him, so he tried to kill David.

ASK *What do you think David did?*

SAY David hid from Saul. Then one night, when Saul and his soldiers were nearby, David and a friend crept into Saul's camp and took Saul's water jug and spear while the king and his men were asleep.

ASK *Why do you think David took Saul's water jug and spear?*

SAY David wanted to teach Saul a lesson. When Saul realized that David could have killed him but didn't, Saul was very sorry that he had treated him so badly. David returned Saul's spear and water jug, and then Saul blessed David. For a time, the king stopped trying to harm the young man, and David continued to trust God to protect him.

☆Let's Play

Think of a person or object familiar to the children from the Bible story. Tell clues so the children can guess the person or object. For example, say **"I'm thinking of a young man. He took care of some animals. He played a musical instrument. God chose him to be the next king of Israel."** After each clue, pause for children to guess the answer. Give a sticker to the child who correctly guesses the answer *(David)*. Then move on to the next person or thing from the story. Provide simple clues for the following: Samuel, Saul, soldiers, water jug, spear.

☆Let's Sing

Listen to and sing "Jesus Is My Great Protector." *Younger Elementary Vol. 2* CD Songbook, p. 7

1 Samuel 26

© GCP www.gcp.org
OK to photocopy for church and home use

Nathan told King David about God's promise.
2 Samuel 7

☆Let's Talk

SAY When David was 30 years old, he became king over Israel. David trusted God to help him lead the people wisely. David began to think about building a house for God, a temple.

ASK *What did the prophet Nathan tell David?*

SAY God sent Nathan to tell David that he didn't want his people to build a temple just yet. But God made a promise to David. He said that he would build a house for David. God wasn't talking about a real house. He was promising that Israel's kings would always come from David's household, his family. God was promising that the Savior, Jesus, would be born into David's family. King Jesus would live and reign forever!

SAY I wonder how David felt when he found out about God's promise . . .

SAY When David heard what God had promised, he was thankful and praised God. He knew that God would do as he said. David had learned that God always keeps his promises!

☆Let's Print

Print the word *Promises* and the letters *P* and *p* on the **chalkboard or poster board**. Let the children use the chalkboard or poster board to copy your writing for handwriting practice and to keep God's promises on their minds!

As they work, talk about some of God's promises to his people they've learned about from Bible stories.

☆Let's Sing

Sing "We Thank Thee, Loving Father." Then sing this additional verse and do the motions.

Preschool Vol. 1 CD track 21
Songbook, p. 28

We thank Thee, loving Father, *(raise both arms)*
For your promises today. *(open hands as a book, the Bible)*
We praise you for the Savior, *(form cross with two index fingers)*
Help us trust you and obey! *(fold hands, as if in prayer)*

King David was sorry for his sin.

2 Samuel 11–12; Psalm 51

King David was sorry for his sin.
2 Samuel 11–12; Psalm 51

☆ Let's Talk

SAY David was a good king. He obeyed and served God. But David was not sinless. One time David committed a very bad sin against God. David had one of his best soldiers killed so he could take the man's wife, Bathsheba, as his own. God was not pleased. God sent the prophet Nathan to speak to David about his sin.

ASK Look at the picture of King David. *What does it show?*

SAY When Nathan spoke to David, the king recognized that he had disobeyed God and he felt very sorry for his sins. He wrote a psalm that tells what he did and how he felt.

ASK *What do you think David said in the psalm he wrote?*

SAY King David asked God to forgive him. He asked God to make him clean inside and give him back the joy he had lost because of his wrongdoing.

ASK *What do you think God did?*

SAY God forgave him and made David's heart glad again.

☆ Let's Play

Play this game to help the children understand that when they ask Jesus to forgive their sin, he does it. Stand in a circle. Ask, **"Whom does Jesus forgive?"** Then roll or toss a ball to a child and say, **"Jesus forgives** (child's name).**"** The child you name catches the **ball** and says, **"Jesus forgives** (child's name)**"** as he throws the ball to another child. Continue until each child has had a turn.

☆ Let's Pray

Gather for a responsive prayer. Explain that when you say each phrase, the children are to say, "Thank you, dear Lord." At the end, everyone will say, "Amen."

Leader: Lord, we know that you love us and take care of us.
Children: Thank you, dear Lord.
Leader: You forgive us when we do wrong things and confess them.
Children: Thank you, dear Lord.
Leader: You make our hearts clean and restore our joy.
Children: Thank you, dear Lord.
Leader: Please help us to trust and obey you. We pray in Jesus' name . . .
All: Amen.

The queen of Sheba visited King Solomon.
1 Kings 3, 10

The queen of Sheba visited King Solomon.

1 Kings 3, 10

☆ Let's Talk

SAY After King David died, Solomon became the next ruler over Israel. God knew that Solomon loved him and wanted to obey him. God told Solomon to ask him for whatever he wanted God to give him.

ASK *What do you think Solomon asked God for?*

SAY Solomon did not ask God for money or jewelry or to make him popular. Solomon asked God to give him wisdom to rule over God's people. God answered Solomon's prayer. Soon everyone thought that Solomon was a great king. He helped people do what was right, he built a beautiful temple for prayer and worship, and he became very rich and important. Solomon did not forget that his wisdom, wealth, and fame were gifts from God.

ASK *What do you see in the picture?*

SAY The queen of Sheba came to visit Solomon. She brought him gifts from her own country and asked him hard questions. He answered all her questions, showed her his beautiful palace, and gave her a wonderful meal. Before she left, she praised God for making Solomon a wise king over Israel. And he sent her off with many royal gifts!

☆ Let's Act

Explain that being wise means not only *knowing* what is right but *doing* what is right. Then let the children act out situations where they must choose the right thing. (Examples: obeying when told to pick up toys, going to bed without complaining, listening to the teacher in Sunday school, sharing with a friend on the playground, not begging at the store with mom, etc.)

Remind children that Jesus helps us know and do what is right. We can ask Jesus for wisdom and he will give it to us. God's Word teaches us how to live in a way that pleases him. And Jesus forgives when we sin and say we are sorry!

☆ Let's Use It Right

❶ Place the following items in a **bag: video game, pack of crayons, Bible, box of raisins, seed package, a treat for a pet, a ball,** and so on.

❷ Let the children take turns reaching into the bag and pulling out an item without looking. Children will tell why they are thankful for the item and how they can choose to use it the right way. When everyone has an item, encourage volunteers to offer a sentence prayer thanking God for what they are holding.

God provided food for Elijah.
1 Kings 17

☆Let's Talk

SAY King Ahab, a very wicked king, was mad at God's prophet Elijah. God told the prophet to go away and hide by the Kerith stream, where he would be safe from the king.

ASK Look at the picture. *What do you see?*

SAY Elijah trusted God and did what he said. Once he got there, ravens brought him bread and meat to eat every day. He had plenty of water to drink from the stream.

ASK *Who took care of Elijah?*

SAY God took care of Elijah, as the prophet knew he would. After a while, God told Elijah to travel to a small town. Again, Elijah trusted and obeyed God. When he arrived, the prophet stayed with a widow and her son. The woman had hardly any food, but Elijah told her that God would provide for them. And each day there was enough food for them all.

ASK *Who took care of the widow, her son, and Elijah?*

SAY God kept his promise to provide for them. And when the widow's son died, Elijah asked the Lord to bring the son back to life. When the Lord made the boy alive again, the thankful widow knew that Elijah was God's prophet and that what he said and did came from God himself. Elijah spoke God's word faithfully during a time when many of the Israelites were disobeying God.

☆Let's Do

Print the words *trust* and *obey* in large dotted letters on a sheet of **paper**. Make **photocopies** and let children trace the letters with **crayons**. As they work, talk about what it means to trust and obey Jesus as well as parents, teachers, and others who may be in charge of us.

☆Let's Sing

Sing "I Will Follow," a simple song of trust and obedience.

Younger Elementary Vol. 2 CD
Songbook, p. 7

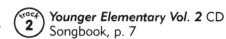

God sent fire to the altar when Elijah prayed.
1 Kings 18

God sent fire to the altar when Elijah prayed.
1 Kings 18

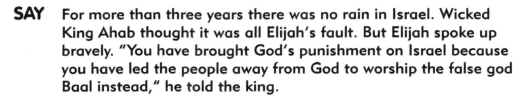

☆Let's Talk and Wonder

SAY For more than three years there was no rain in Israel. Wicked King Ahab thought it was all Elijah's fault. But Elijah spoke up bravely. "You have brought God's punishment on Israel because you have led the people away from God to worship the false god Baal instead," he told the king.

SAY Elijah told King Ahab to gather the people and all the false prophets on Mount Carmel so everyone could see that God is the true and living God, not Baal. So everyone gathered on the mountain to see what would take place.

SAY I wonder what happened when Baal's followers called on Baal . . .

SAY The followers of Baal offered a sacrifice and asked Baal to send fire to burn up the offering. They called all day, but nothing happened. That's because Baal wasn't real. He was just a false god and had no power.

SAY Elijah prepared an offering for the Lord. He poured water all over the offering and the altar. Then he prayed.

ASK *What do you see in the picture?*

SAY After Elijah prayed, God sent fire! It burned up the offering, the wood, the altar, and every drop of water! The people were amazed at the miracle and fell on the ground and cried, "The Lord, he is God." Then God sent rain to Israel!

☆Let's Make and Say

1. Make **photocopies** of the coloring picture and mount them on **poster board**. Provide **blue glitter glue** and **strips of yellow, orange, and red tissue paper**.

2. Let children drip blue glitter glue on and around the altar to remind them of the water that Elijah poured all over the offering.

3. Then stick strips of tissue paper to the glitter glue to remember that God sent fire, which burned up the wet altar and everything on and around it! Point out that God is powerful and trustworthy.

Elijah told King Ahab that he sinned.

1 Kings 21

Elijah told King Ahab that he sinned.

1 Kings 21 (Exodus 20:16)

☆Let's Talk

SAY King Ahab wanted a vineyard that belonged to a man named Naboth. But Naboth wouldn't part with it because it had been in his family for many years.

ASK *What do you think King Ahab did?*

SAY King Ahab was so mad he went to bed and pouted! His wife Jezebel told him not to worry about it. She would see to it that he got the vineyard he wanted.

SAY Jezebel made some troublemakers lie about Naboth. They accused him of speaking against God and the king. So Naboth was dragged away and stoned to death. When Jezebel told Ahab that Naboth was dead, the king went down to claim Naboth's vineyard as his own.

ASK *What do you see in the picture?*

SAY The prophet Elijah told Ahab that God would bring judgment on the king and his wife because they broke God's law—the ninth commandment—to get Naboth's vineyard. When Ahab heard what God's prophet said, he was very sorry for what he had done. God told Elijah that since Ahab was truly sorry for his sin, judgment would not come during Ahab's lifetime, but it would come to Ahab's household after he died.

☆Let's Listen

Listen to "Ten Commandments Song" while coloring. The ninth commandment tells us to not lie. Jesus is the only one who never lied. He died to forgive our sin. When we lie, we can confess our sin and Jesus forgives us.

☆Let's Play

Play *God's Word Says*, which is like *Simon Says*. The children may do the actions below only if you say the words **"God's Word says"** before the command. If you don't say "God's Word says," they must stand still. Keep a quick pace while you play.

- *God's Word says* tell the truth. Take two steps forward.
- Do unkind things. Make a face.
- *God's Word says* trust and obey God. Make a cross with both arms.
- Blame someone else for a wrong thing that you did. Point to your neighbor.
- *God's Word says* love others. Hold hands with a friend.

© GCP www.gcp.org
OK to photocopy for church and home use

Naaman washed in the river and was healed.
2 Kings 5

Naaman washed in the river and was healed.
2 Kings 5

☆Let's Talk

SAY Naaman, the commander of the Syrian army, had a skin disease called leprosy. There was a young servant girl from Israel in his household. She knew who could help Naaman.

ASK *Who do you think it was?*

SAY The girl said that Naaman should go and see the prophet Elisha. She knew that God could cure her master of his leprosy through Elisha. The young servant girl trusted in God and his power to save and heal.

ASK *What do you think happened when Naaman arrived at Elisha's house?*

SAY Elisha's servant came out with a message from the prophet. He told Naaman to wash himself seven times in the Jordan River to be healed. Naaman became angry and turned to leave. He was mad that the prophet didn't come out and speak to him, and he didn't want to wash in the muddy Jordan River. But Naaman's servants advised him to do what Elisha said.

ASK *What happened when Naaman washed seven times in the Jordan River?*

SAY When Naaman came out of the river, he saw that the leprosy was completely gone! He went back to Elisha and said, "Now I know that there is no God in all the earth except the God of Israel." Elisha blessed Naaman and sent him on his way. God had healed him of his leprosy, and Naaman thanked and praised God!

☆Let's Make and Mention

Tape a length of **shelf paper** to the table and set out **markers** and **glitter glue**. Guide the children to make a story mural of the servant girl and the healing of Naaman. As children create scenes from the story, talk about how great and wonderful God is. Mention ways children can show their faith in their great Savior, Jesus. Mount the finished mural on the wall.

☆Let's Praise

Remind children that God healed Naaman, and Naaman was thankful and praised God. Let them praise God for the good things he gives them. Let volunteers take turns completing this sentence: **"I praise God for . . . ."**

King Josiah read God's Word to the people.

2 Kings 22–23

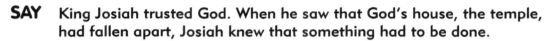

☆Let's Talk

SAY King Josiah trusted God. When he saw that God's house, the temple, had fallen apart, Josiah knew that something had to be done.

ASK *What do you think Josiah did?*

SAY Josiah told the priests through a messenger, "Take the money collected from the people and use it to repair the temple of the Lord. Hire workers, buy wood and stone, and get the work done!"

ASK While cleaning up the mess, the workers found something very special. *What was it?*

SAY The workers found a dusty copy of God's law, part of the Bible. It had not been read for many years. When the priest read the words on the scroll to the king, he became very upset. "We have not obeyed God the way we should. We have not pleased God," Josiah said sadly. Then he called together all God's people.

ASK Look at the picture. *What do you see?*

SAY Everyone came to hear God's law that was written on the scroll found in the temple. They listened carefully as it was read. All the people said, "We will obey God's Word." King Josiah turned to the Lord with his whole heart and he led the people of Israel to do the same!

☆Let's Put Away and Say

1. Talk about the importance of listening to God's Word. Then talk about ways we can help take good care of our church, the place where God's people gather to worship him.

2. Next, have the children name some places and things that need to be cleaned up (table, chairs, crayons, papers, and so on). Let everyone pick a place or thing to help with. Then assign tasks so that all children are involved in cleanup activities.

☆Let's Sing

Sing these words and do motions to the tune *The Farmer in the Dell*.

1. The B–I–B–L–E,
The B–I–B–L–E,
I'll listen to your Word,
The B–I–B–L–E. *(hold hands open like a book)*

2. The B–I–B–L–E,
The B–I–B–L–E,
Help me obey your Word,
The B–I–B–L–E. *(fold hands, as if in prayer)*

King Asa obeyed God's Word.
2 Chronicles 14–15

King Asa obeyed God's Word.
2 Chronicles 14–15

☆Let's Talk

ASK *What do you see in the picture?*

SAY King Asa told the people of Judah to seek the Lord their God and obey his laws and commands. He led them in turning their hearts toward God, and there was peace in the land for 10 years. Then something dreadful happened. A powerful army came near and was ready to fight King Asa and his troops.

ASK *What do you think King Asa did?*

SAY King Asa prayed. He called on the Lord for help and victory, and God answered his prayers. God struck down the enemy right in front of King Asa and his men. The frightened soldiers ran, and Asa and his troops chased them away.

☆Let's Play

Have all the children stand on one side of the room while you stand on the other side. Say a command below. Have the children listen and obey it. As they are moving forward, say, **"Freeze!"** If a child doesn't freeze his position, he has to go back to the starting line. Keep going until a child reaches you.

- God is pleased when we obey his Word. *Tiptoe forward.*
- We need Jesus' help to obey God's Word. *Skip forward.*
- We can trust the Lord for the help we need to obey his Word. *Hop forward.*
- Thank God for helping us trust and obey him. *Run forward.*

☆Let's Sing a Prayer

Sing this prayer about obeying God's Word to the tune *Jingle Bells*. Encourage children to follow your motions.

Help me, Lord, help me Lord, *(fold hands in prayer)*
Help me to obey.
Order my steps by your Word, *(open hands as if a Bible)*
Guard my heart, I pray. *(place hands over heart)*
Help me, Lord, help me, Lord, *(fold hands in prayer)*
Help me to obey.
Let me always trust in you, *(point up)*
So I can walk God's way! *(walk in place)*

King Joash repaired the temple.
2 Chronicles 22–24

☆Let's Talk

SAY Joash was made king of Israel when he was just a boy. His Uncle Jehoiada, a wise priest, helped him rule. When Joash grew up, he decided to repair the temple of God.

ASK *What do you see in the picture?*

SAY Workers were hired to make the temple like new again. Then King Joash and the people worshiped God at the temple. But when his uncle died, Joash turned away from God and worshiped false gods.

ASK *What do you think happened next?*

SAY God sent Zechariah, the son of Jehoiada, to speak to the people. "Since you have stopped following God, he will no longer be with you," Zechariah said. King Joash and the Israelites did not want to hear Zechariah's message, so they stoned him to death.

ASK *What do you think happened to Joash?*

SAY God punished Joash. The king was wounded in battle, and then his own servants killed him because of what he had done to Zechariah.

SAY Many years later, God sent Jesus to be our Savior, just as he promised. Jesus gives those who trust in him new hearts that want to keep following Jesus. Jesus will never leave those who believe in him.

☆Let's Build

Set out **blocks** and **toy people**. Build a church. The children can pretend that the toy people are carpenters, bricklayers, and metalworkers. When the church is finished, pretend some toy people are going in to worship Jesus.

☆Let's Sing

Prayerfully sing this song to the tune *London Bridge Is Falling Down*.

Preschool Vol. 2 CD

> Help us trust you and obey,
> Every day, every day.
> Help us trust you and obey,
> Lord, we pray!

God's people returned to Jerusalem and rebuilt the temple.

Ezra 1, 3

God's people returned to Jerusalem and rebuilt the temple.

Ezra 1, 3

☆Let's Talk

SAY God was ready for his people to leave Babylon and go back to Jerusalem. So he caused the king to let them go. The king returned all the things that had been taken from the temple many years before. He also gave God's people all that they needed to start life again in their own land. Then the people made the long journey back home.

ASK *After they had settled in their own towns, what do you think God's people did?*

SAY They got together in Jerusalem. They rebuilt the altar, offered sacrifices to the Lord, and gave money to rebuild the temple. When the foundation of the temple was in place, the people gathered around.

SAY The people took their places to praise the Lord for being powerful and in charge, and for being loving and faithful. He had kept his promise to bring his people back to their homeland. And now led by the priests, the people sang, shouted, and played musical instruments to the Lord. "He is good," they said. "His steadfast love endures forever to Israel!"

Jesus' love for his children will last forever, too! His children will live with him forever. We can praise Jesus for his love!

☆Let's Pretend

Ask the children to stand. Tell them to pretend to be the children of Israel. Lead them in doing the motions suggested by the action words in italic.

1. We're *traveling* back to Jerusalem. It's a long, *tiring* walk!
2. We're *happy* to be home. Let's *unpack* our things.
3. Let's *hurry* over to Jerusalem!
4. We're *giving* our offerings so the temple can be rebuilt.
5. Let's *build* the foundation of the temple.
6. Let's *shout* to the Lord.
7. Let's *sing* God's praises for sending Jesus to be our Savior.
8. Let's *blow* our trumpets and *sound* our cymbals.

☆Let's Pray

Dear God, thank you for loving us. Thank you that you are powerful and that you are in charge. Thank you for being faithful, for keeping your promises. We praise you for your goodness. Help us trust and obey you more and more each day. In Jesus' name, Amen.

Ezra taught God's Word.

Ezra 7; Nehemiah 8–10

Ezra taught God's Word.
Ezra 7; Nehemiah 8–10

☆Let's Talk

SAY Ezra the priest lived in Babylon, but he wanted to return to Jerusalem to teach God's Word to the people there. Guess what? The king of Persia sent Ezra a letter telling him to go back to Jerusalem. He promised to give Ezra everything he needed for the trip. He promised to send gifts, and he told Ezra to rule the people wisely and teach them the law of God.

SAY I wonder how Ezra felt after reading the king's letter . . .

SAY Ezra praised God for bringing all this about! Then the priest and many Israelites returned to Jerusalem. When they arrived in the city after many months of traveling, large crowds gathered in the streets to hear God's Word.

ASK What do you see in the picture?

SAY Ezra read God's Word to all the people. Ezra praised the Lord, and the people said, "Amen! Amen!" Then they bowed down and worshiped the Lord.

SAY The people listened as Ezra read and explained God's law to them. They were sorry that they had forgotten God's Word and disobeyed it for so long. They confessed their sin and agreed to obey God's Word. Then all the people celebrated with glad hearts!

☆Let's Make and Say

1 Explain that in Bible times, God's Word was written on a scroll, a rolled-up piece of leather. Ezra would have read to the people from a scroll.

2 Make a scroll. Get a long strip of **butcher paper**, about 45" long and 10" wide. Using **tape or glue**, attach each end to a **15" dowel**. Print this prayer in the middle of the scroll: **Dear God, thank you for your Word. Help me to listen to and learn your Word. Help me obey it and tell others what it says about Jesus. In Jesus' name, Amen.** Have the children draw pictures of themselves on the scroll. Then roll up the scroll.

3 Gather the children around you. Have someone unroll the scroll. Talk about God's wonderful Word, the Bible, that tells us about our Savior, Jesus. Then lead the group in saying the prayer written on it.

Esther asked King Xerxes to save God's people.

Esther 1–10

Esther asked King Xerxes to save God's people.
Esther 1–10

☆Let's Talk

SAY An order was sent throughout the Persian kingdom that all Jews were to be put to death. Queen Esther's Uncle Mordecai told her to go to powerful King Xerxes and ask him to spare God's people. Esther told Mordecai to gather together all Jews and have them pray about the matter. Even for the queen, it was dangerous to go before the king without permission.

ASK Look at the picture. *What do you see?*

SAY After Esther, her uncle, and the rest of God's people in the Persian kingdom finished praying, Esther went before King Xerxes. She invited the king and Haman, the chief of all his nobles, to a feast.

ASK *What do you think happened at the feast?*

SAY When Esther, Xerxes, and Haman were eating together, Esther asked the king to spare her life and the lives of her people. The king was furious when he learned that it was wicked Haman who had plotted to kill all Jews in the kingdom. He commanded that Haman be put to death right away. Then the king made a new law.

ASK *What do you think the new law said?*

SAY The new law said that the Jews could fight for their lives if anyone tried to harm them. On the day they were all supposed to die, God's people were victorious. They had a wonderful holiday celebrating what God had done for them through Esther and her uncle.

☆Let's Celebrate and Say

Spread a large, colorful **quilt** on the floor. Sit in a circle and have a "feast." Serve **cheese slices, fruit slices, grapes, pita crackers,** and a **drink**. (Be aware of allergies.) As children eat, remind them that God put Esther in the king's palace and used her to save his people, the Jews. Say sentence prayers thanking God for saving his people back then and for saving us today through Jesus, his Son.

☆Let's Sing

Sing either "Jesus Bids Us Shine" or "Be Strong." Both songs are found in *Younger Elementary Vol. 2* Songbook and on the CD.

"Make a joyful noise to the Lord, all the earth!"

Psalm 100

"Make a joyful noise to the Lord, all the earth!"
Psalm 100

☆Let's Talk

ASK *What are some of the things you like best that God created? How does God take care of the things you named?*

SAY God made the world and everything it. He cares for everything he made. We ought to praise him for being such a wonderful Creator! He deserves our praise for being our faithful God. He deserves our praise for sending Jesus to be our Savior. He deserves our praise for saving us, keeping us, and leading us.

☆Let's Listen and Move

Psalm 100 tells the whole world to worship the Lord because of who he is. Explain to your children that God looks after us because we belong to him. The psalm pictures us as the sheep that God tends. Sheep need a shepherd to care for them and lead them. We praise God because he is faithful to his own!

Invite the children to sit in a circle and listen as you read Psalm 100 from the **Bible** out loud. Read slowly and expressively.

☆Let's Make

Get a sheet of **poster board** and write in large letters *Jesus is my Shepherd*. Gather some **sheep stickers** (you should be able to find some at your local Christian bookstore or online). Let each child place a sheep sticker around the words. Write each child's name under his or her sticker. When the poster is finished, say the caption aloud and read and point to every child's name.

☆Let's Pray

Lead the children in saying this prayer, repeating after you phrase by phrase.

> Dear God,
> Thank you that you made us and take care of us.
> Thank you for sending Jesus to die on a cross for our sins.
> Thank you that you never stop being faithful to us.
> Help us to trust and obey you.
> We praise you for being so wonderful!
> In Jesus' name, Amen.

Psalm 100

© GCP www.gcp.org
OK to photocopy for church and home use

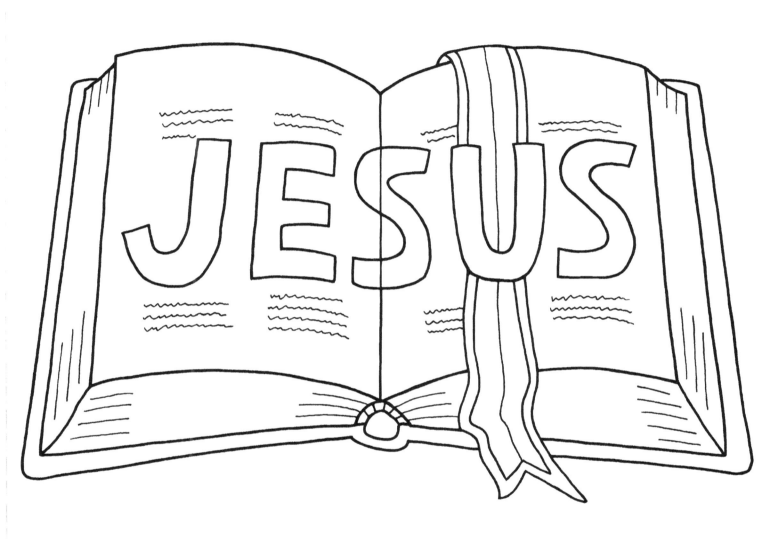

God's Word is about his Son.

Isaiah 40–53; Micah 5, 7

 **God's Word is about his Son.**
Isaiah 40–53; Micah 5, 7

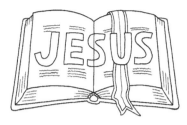

☆Let's Talk

SAY Isaiah was a prophet of God. He lived a long time ago and was a preacher of God's message. Isaiah also wrote down God's words. Isaiah told the people to prepare the way for the promised Son of God.

SAY Around the same time that Isaiah lived, another prophet named Micah was sent by God to preach to the people and write down God's message. Micah told the people that he was watching and waiting for the coming of God the Savior too. Many, many years before the Savior was born, Micah wrote down the city the Messiah would be born in—Bethlehem.

ASK *Did God keep his promise?*

SAY The New Testament tells us that God kept his promise and that the Savior *did* come. Jesus, God's Son, was born in Bethlehem, just as Micah had written. And everything that Isaiah wrote about Jesus was true too.

ASK *Why did Jesus come?*

SAY Jesus came to die on the cross for the sins of God's people. Our wonderful God kept his promise to send the Savior to die for our sins. We learn about God's great truths and promises in his Word, the Bible! The Bible is about Jesus!

☆Let's Sing

Sing "Wonderful Words of Life." *Younger Elementary Vol. 1* CD
Songbook, p. 21

☆Let's Make and Say

① Print **"I have stored up your word in my heart"** from Psalm 119:11 in block letters on a sheet of **paper**. Make a **photocopy** for each child. Let each child color the verse and add borders of **Bible stickers** or Bible story drawings. Then mount each page on **construction paper**.

② Talk about how thankful we are that we have God's Word to teach us about God, his promises, and his Son, our Savior. Let children display their Bible verse posters as you say the words from Psalm 119:11 together.

Jeremiah preached God's message.

Jeremiah 37–39

Jeremiah preached God's message.
Jeremiah 37–39

☆Let's Talk

SAY Jeremiah the prophet was willing to obey the Lord even when it was hard. The Lord had promised to lead and protect Jeremiah, and the prophet believed his promise. God told Jeremiah to tell his people that he was going to send the Babylonians to punish them because they had once again turned away from serving God.

ASK *What do you think God's people did when Jeremiah told them what God said?*

SAY The people became angry and wouldn't listen to the prophet. When the Babylonians came, Jeremiah warned God's people that they would die if they stayed in Jerusalem. They beat Jeremiah and threw him in prison.

ASK *What did Jeremiah do?*

SAY Jeremiah didn't stop speaking the truth and obeying the Lord. "He is full of bad news," the people complained. So Jeremiah was put in a deep well to die. The king called for Jeremiah, but the king still chose to disobey God's message. After that, Jerusalem was destroyed, just like God said to Jeremiah.

SAY Even so, God protected Jeremiah from harm and didn't turn away from his people. God promised to send the Savior and turn their hearts back to him so that they would want to obey him.

☆Let's Play

Gather **two bathrobes, two towels,** and **two pieces of string or rope.** Divide the class into two teams. Line up both teams behind a starting line with one set of clothing in front of the first person in each team. At your signal, both players put on the bathrobe and then put on the towel as a headdress, tying the string to hold it in place. Each player then runs to a designated turning point—perhaps named "Jeremiah's deep well"—and back, and then takes off the outfit. Each team member repeats this pattern until everyone has had a turn. The first team to finish wins!

☆Let's Pray

Point out that Jesus wants us to obey him. He will always be with his followers. Then pray, asking Jesus to give the children strength and courage to obey him, even when it's hard.

Daniel and his three friends were brought to the king.

Daniel 1

Daniel and his three friends were brought to the king.
Daniel 1

☆Let's Talk and Wonder

SAY The king of Babylon came and captured many of God's people and took them back to Babylon with him. They now had to live in a strange land among people who did not worship God.

SAY I wonder how God's people felt when they were living in Babylon . . .

SAY The king of Babylon wanted some smart, young Israelite men to serve in his palace. So Daniel and his three friends were brought to the king's court and their Jewish names were changed to Babylonian names. Daniel became Belteshazzar.

SAY Daniel and his friends continued to obey God's laws while they were being trained to serve the king. And at the end of three years, the four strong, healthy young men had learned everything they were taught at the king's court. They were presented to the king.

SAY The king was amazed at how smart they were, how good they looked, and how much they knew. God had taken loving care of his four obedient followers. He protected them and gave them what they needed to serve him in Babylon. Daniel and his friends were willing to trust and obey God in every situation because they knew God loved them!

☆Let's Sing

Lead children in singing the following song to the tune *Jesus Loves the Little Children*.

❶ God loved Daniel and his friends,
God loved Daniel and his friends.
They trusted him each day,
He helped them obey.
God loved Daniel and his friends
all the way!

❷ God loves all the little children,
All the children who are his.
We trust him each day,
He helps us obey.
God loves all the little children
who are his!

☆Let's Listen

Slowly say or read Psalm 23 expressively as the children listen.

Daniel 1

© GCP www.gcp.org
OK to photocopy for church and home use

God protected Shadrach, Meshach, and Abednego.
Daniel 3

☆Let's Talk

SAY The king of Babylon did not love God. He had a huge gold statue made and ordered everyone to bow down and worship it. If they didn't obey, they would be thrown into a blazing fire.

ASK *Did everyone obey the king?*

SAY No. Shadrach, Meshach, and Abednego said, "We will not worship the statue you made or serve your gods. If we're thrown into the fire, the God we serve is able to save us. But even if he does not, we will remain obedient to him. He is the only true and powerful God and he takes care of his children."

ASK *What happened to the three friends who loved God?*

SAY The king made sure the fire was hotter than ever and had Shadrach, Meshach, and Abednego tied up and thrown into the furnace. But then the king quickly jumped to his feet. "Didn't we throw three men into the fire? There are four men walking around in there. One looks like an angel!" the surprised king said.

ASK *What do you think happened next?*

SAY The king called the men to come out of the fire. They were not burnt or harmed in any way. The king said, "Praise be to the God of Shadrach, Meshach, and Abednego. They trusted in the Lord and he rescued them!" Then the king honored the three friends because of their faithfulness to God!

☆Let's Make

Make touch-and-feel pictures. Make a **photocopy** of the coloring page for each child. Mount it on **poster board**. Set out **red** and **yellow tissue paper** and **glue**. Tear strips of the tissue paper and glue them to the flames in the picture. Glue on other items such as **rice, beans, cotton, glitter,** and **fabric**. As the children work, talk about God's power and how he protects his children in big and small ways.

☆Let's Pray

Lead the group in saying this prayer.

> Dear God, thank you that you are more powerful than anyone or anything. Thank you for taking care of us. Help us trust and obey you. In Jesus' name, Amen.

Daniel read the strange words on the wall.
Daniel 5

Daniel read the strange words on the wall.
Daniel 5

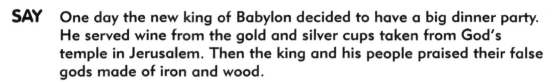

☆Let's Talk

SAY One day the new king of Babylon decided to have a big dinner party. He served wine from the gold and silver cups taken from God's temple in Jerusalem. Then the king and his people praised their false gods made of iron and wood.

ASK *What do you think happened next at the dinner party?*

SAY All at once, writing appeared on the palace wall. The frightened king called for his wise men. "If you can read this writing," he said. "I will give you a great reward."

ASK *Were the wise men able to read the words?*

SAY The wise men couldn't tell the king what the words meant, so the troubled king called for God's prophet Daniel.

ASK *What do you see in the picture?*

SAY Daniel explained the words to the king. He said that the king had not honored God. The king had refused to believe that God is in control of everything. He had taken the holy cups from God's house and had worshiped false gods. For these reasons, God had sent the message of judgment on the wall. That night the disobedient king was killed and his kingdom was destroyed. God took care of his people and gave Daniel a very important position in the new kingdom.

☆Let's Make

Tape a length of **shelf paper** to the wall. Let the children call out "messages" that tell about God and his power and care in our lives. For example, they might say "God is in control" or "God cares for me" or "God helps me obey him." Print each message on the paper. When children have finished, go over each message and talk about our wonderful God, who is in charge!

☆Let's Sing

Sing "Love the Lord with All Your Heart and Soul." *Younger Elementary Vol. 2* CD Songbook, p. 28

God protected Daniel from the lions.
Daniel 6

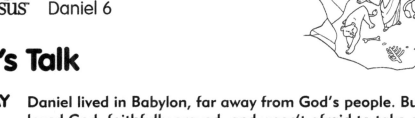

☆Let's Talk

SAY Daniel lived in Babylon, far away from God's people. But Daniel loved God, faithfully prayed, and wasn't afraid to take a stand for what was right. Daniel had an important job. He worked for the king, who liked Daniel and gave him an important job over the whole kingdom. But the king made a new rule saying that for 30 days no one could pray to a god or ask anyone but the king for anything. If anyone broke the rule, he would be thrown into the lions' den.

ASK *What did Daniel do?*

SAY Daniel continued to pray to God. Some men who wanted to get Daniel in trouble told the king that Daniel had disobeyed the king's rule. So the king threw Daniel into the lions' den. "May your God, whom you serve continually, rescue you!" the king said to Daniel.

ASK *What do you see in the picture?*

SAY The next morning, the king hurried to the lions' den. He called out to Daniel and discovered that he was safe. "My God sent his angel," Daniel said, "and shut the lions' mouths, and they have not harmed me." The king was very happy and gave orders to lift Daniel out of the den. Then the king wrote a letter to everyone telling them to honor the living God, who saved Daniel from the lions and whose powerful reign lasts forever!

☆Let's Pretend

Set out **blocks, toy people,** and **lions.** Let the children act out the story of Daniel and the lions' den. They can build a den and put the animals inside. They can show Daniel with the lions. They can act out the king's morning visit to the den and his joyful visit to Daniel.

☆Let's Sing and Worship

Play "God Is Always Near Me." The children can listen, sing, or do actions.

Toddler Sing-Along With Me CD track 7
Songbook, p. 10

After singing, help the children make worship statements. They can take turns completing this sentence: **"I praise God because he cares for me when . . ."**

Daniel 6

© GCP www.gcp.org
OK to photocopy for church and home use

Jonah spent three days inside the big fish.
Jonah 1–4

Jonah spent three days inside the big fish.
Jonah 1–4

☆Let's Talk

SAY God told Jonah to go to Nineveh. God wanted Jonah to preach his Word there. But Jonah didn't want to talk to the people of Nineveh because they were God's enemies. So he tried to run away from God's call.

ASK *Where did Jonah go and what happened?*

SAY Jonah got on a ship that was sailing far away from Nineveh. God sent a big storm to stop Jonah from running away. Jonah told the frightened sailors on the battered ship to throw him over the side and the storm would go away. They did as Jonah said and the sea became calm. The sailors knew that God had done it. They feared and worshiped God!

ASK *What did God provide for Jonah in the sea?*

SAY God sent a big fish to swallow Jonah. For three days he was inside the big fish. When Jonah prayed to God for help, the fish spit him out onto dry land. Again, God told Jonah to go to Nineveh and preach his message there. This time, Jonah obeyed God and went to Nineveh!

☆Let's Play

1. Use **masking tape** to outline a large fish shape on the floor.
2. Have the children line up on one side of the room to play this version of *Mother, May I?*
3. You stand across the room in "Nineveh" and give commands to one child at a time such as, **"Take two hops toward Nineveh."** The child should respond with the words, **"I'll obey what you say"** before doing what is commanded. If any player does a command without saying, "I'll obey what you say," the player must sit inside the big fish until the game is over. Continue giving commands to the players one at a time until everyone either makes it to Nineveh or is "swallowed" by the big fish!
4. Remind the children that we all disobey. That's why we need Jesus. Jesus is the only one who never disobeyed; he obeyed perfectly. He died to forgive our disobedience and give us a new heart that wants to trust and obey.

☆Let's Pray

Lead the children in saying this prayer.

> Dear God, thank you for loving us and being with us wherever we go. Help us to trust you and do what you say. In Jesus' name, Amen.

Micah said the Messiah would be born in Bethlehem.

Micah 5:2

Micah said the Messiah would be born in Bethlehem.
Micah 5:2

☆Let's Talk

SAY Long before Jesus was born, God promised to send the Savior to save his people from their sins. He made that promise to Adam and Eve, Abraham, Isaiah, Micah, and others.

ASK *What do you see in the picture?*

SAY The man in the picture is the prophet Micah. When he told about the coming of the promised Savior, he even said the place of his birth—Bethlehem, the city that you see in the picture.

ASK *What else did God say about the promised Savior through his people in the Old Testament?*

SAY God said that the Savior would come from King David's family. He said that the Savior would come as a baby. He would be called Wonderful Counselor, Mighty God, Everlasting Father, and Prince of Peace.

ASK *Did God keep his promise?*

SAY God kept his promise by sending Jesus, his Son, to die for our sins.

☆Let's Make

Give each child a sheet of **red construction paper.** Have the children draw a heart. Provide **popped popcorn** and **glue.** Glue the popcorn along the outline while talking about God's great love. *Say* **God loved us first and he never stops loving his children. He sent his Son, Jesus, to save us from our sins. He came to be our Wonderful Counselor, Mighty God, Everlasting Father, and Prince of Peace because of his great love for us!** (Explain what these titles for Jesus mean.)

☆Let's Play and Say

Play this version of *Musical Chairs.* Arrange the chairs (one less than the number of children) in a row or circle. As you play music, the children walk around the chairs. When the music stops, everyone tries to sit down. Have the child left standing thank Jesus for one thing. Continue playing as time allows.

Joseph believed the angel's message about Jesus.
Matthew 1

(His name will be Jesus.)

☆Let's Talk

SAY Joseph wondered if he should get married to Mary. One night an angel brought him a message from God. The angel said, "Take Mary as your wife. The baby that she is expecting is the Son of God. When she gives birth to him, call him Jesus—which means *Savior*—because he will save his people from their sins."

ASK What do you think Joseph did when he heard the message from God?

SAY Joseph believed the angel of the Lord. When the baby was born, Joseph would name him Jesus, just as the angel said. The Savior was coming to save his people. God's people are all those who believe that the Lord Jesus came to be their Savior. They trust in him alone to save them!

☆Let's Echo and Move

1. Sit everyone in a circle. Pat your legs in a slow rhythm. Have the children imitate your actions. Begin speaking rhythmically, accenting the words and syllables in capital letters in the sentence below:

    JE-sus CAME to SAVE his PE-ople FROM their SINS.

2. Children echo the words, using the same rhythm pattern. Vary the activity by clapping hands instead of patting legs.

3. Next, lead the children in doing motions as they affirm this wonderful truth. As you say the words rhythmically, include the following actions:

    Jesus *(point up)* **came to save** *(use arms and hands to make the shape of a cross)* **his people** *(interlock fingers and hold them up)* **from their sins** *(close eyes, fold hands in prayer)*.

☆Let's Pray

Gather the children around you. Have them say each line of this prayer after you.

> Dear God, thank you for sending Jesus to be our Savior.
> Help us to trust him, listen to his Word, and obey him.
> In Jesus' name, Amen.

Mary believed the good news!

Luke 1:26–56

Mary believed the good news!
Luke 1:26–56

☆Let's Talk

ASK *Who do you see in the picture?*

SAY The angel Gabriel told Mary that by a miracle of God she would give birth to a baby boy. He would be God's own Son, the promised Savior. The baby would be named Jesus! Mary is the person in the picture. She believed the message Gabriel brought from God.

ASK *How do you think Mary felt when she heard the good news?*

SAY Mary was very happy that God had blessed her and that he had remembered his promise to his people. She hurried off to visit her cousin Elizabeth, the mother of John. While there, she joyfully praised God for his goodness in a song of praise.

☆Let's Make

Print the following words from Mary's song on a sheet of **paper**: "My soul magnifies the Lord" Luke 1:46. Make a **photocopy** for each child. Let each child color the words and then mount the page on **tagboard or construction paper**. Children will enjoy adding borders made of **glitter glue, rice, popped popcorn,** or **stickers**. Encourage children to hang the poster in a play area at home!

☆Let's Sing and Praise

Invite the children to gather in a circle. Lead them in singing this praise song to the tune *Here We Go Round the Mulberry Bush*. Have them stand and clap as they sing the first verse loudly. Have them sit and fold their hands in prayer as they sing the second verse softly.

Preschool Vol. 2 CD

❶ Thank you, God, for sending your Son,
Sending your Son, sending your Son.
Thank you, God, for sending your Son,
To be the promised Savior.

❷ Give us hearts that trust in you,
Trust in you, trust in you.
Give us hearts that trust in you,
Jesus Christ, our Savior.

John the Baptist was born.

Luke 1:5–25, 57–80

John the Baptist was born.
Luke 1:5–25, 57–80

☆Let's Talk and Wonder

ASK *What does the picture show?*

SAY An angel from God told Zechariah that he and Elizabeth would have a son and they were to name him John. John would get people ready for the coming of the promised Savior. Zechariah did not believe the news. The angel told him that he would not be able to speak until the baby was born. Everyone was glad when Elizabeth gave birth to a son. Zechariah wrote on a tablet, "His name is John." Right away, Zechariah could talk again!

ASK *What did Zechariah say?*

SAY Zechariah praised God. He was thankful that God had sent John, just as he said he would. When John grew up, he would tell everyone to prepare for the coming of God's Son, the Savior.

SAY I wonder how you would have felt if you had been there with Zechariah, Elizabeth, and baby John . . .

☆Let's Act

Let the children act out the story of John's birth with simple props. Bring in **towels** and **scarves** to represent Bible-times clothing for Zechariah, Elizabeth, and their neighbors and relatives. Use a **writing tablet** and **crayons** for Zechariah to write "His name is John." (You may write this out ahead of time.) Bring a **doll** to represent the baby John.

☆Let's Make and Praise

❶ Make praise megaphones. Give each child a brightly colored sheet of **construction paper**. Decorate one side with drawings and **praise stickers**. Then help each child roll up the sheet, artwork side out, into a cone shape. **Tape** the cone closed along the seam. Cut off the bottom and top edges to make it even.

❷ Let your children use their megaphones to shout "Praise be to the Lord" in unison. Then invite them to make praise statements one at a time. Someone can use his megaphone to say, "I praise you, Lord, for loving me." Another child can use her megaphone to say, "I praise you, Lord, for keeping your promises." Give each child a chance to respond.

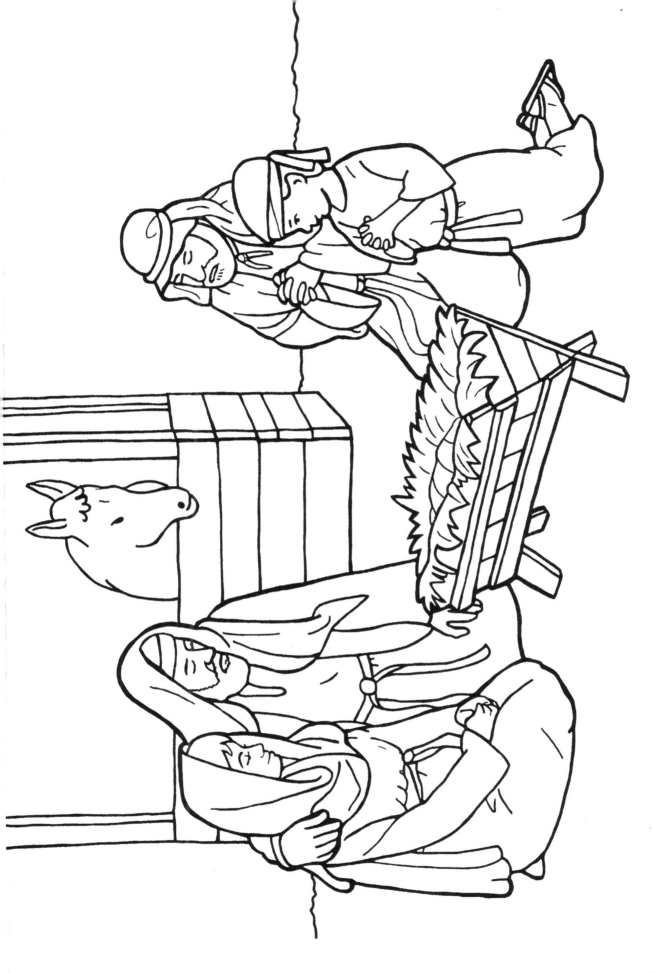

Jesus was born!
Luke 2:1–20

 **Jesus was born!**
Luke 2:1–20

☆Let's Talk

ASK *What do you see in the picture?*

SAY God's Son, the Savior, was born in Bethlehem. Shepherds hurried to the stable, where they found Mary, Joseph, and the baby. When they saw baby Jesus lying in a manger, they were very glad. Everyone looked at the baby with joy!

ASK *What do you think the shepherds did after they saw baby Jesus?*

SAY The shepherds were too excited to keep the good news to themselves. They told everyone that God's Son, the promised Savior, had been born in Bethlehem. As they returned to the fields, the shepherds praised God and thanked him for everything they had seen and heard.

☆Let's Play and Learn

Remind children that Jesus was like other babies in some ways and he was different from other babies in some ways. Then play this learning game. When you name a way that Jesus was like other babies, children must pretend to rock a baby in their arms. When you name a way Jesus was different from other babies, children must point up—as though pointing toward heaven. Be prepared to guide them through this activity.

- Jesus needed a mother to take care of him. *(rock baby in arms)*
- Jesus was God's Son. *(point up)*
- Jesus needed to be held, fed, and changed. *(rock baby in arms)*
- Jesus was born without any sin in his heart. *(point up)*
- Jesus needed to be wrapped in something warm. *(rock baby in arms)*
- Jesus came from heaven to earth to save his people from their sin. *(point up)*

☆Let's Pray

Join hands in a circle. Lead children in saying this prayer, phrase by phrase.

> Dear God, thank you for sending the promised Savior. It was a very special day when Jesus was born. Thank you for loving us enough to send your very own Son to be our Savior. Help us to tell others that Jesus is the Savior! Amen.

The shepherds heard the good news of Jesus' birth.
Luke 2:1–20

☆ Let's Talk and Wonder

ASK *Why do you think God sent his Son, Jesus?*

SAY God sent his own Son, Jesus, to be our Savior. When Jesus was born, angels praised God and shepherds ran to see the baby. Then they went off to spread the good news about the Savior, Christ the Lord.

ASK *Why did Jesus die on the cross?*

SAY Jesus came to die for all our sins. He took the punishment that we deserve so that we could be forgiven. All who trust Jesus for forgiveness of sins are part of God's family.

SAY I wonder what we can say and do to praise God for sending his Son, Jesus, to be our Savior . . .

☆ Let's Sing and Do

Sit in a circle and sing this active song to the tune *Did You Ever See a Lassie?*

❶ God sent his Son, the Savior,
The Savior, the Savior.
God sent his Son, the Savior,
Praise God for his Son! *(clap)*

❷ Jesus died to save me,
To save me, to save me,
Jesus died to save me,
God loves me so! *(hug self)*

❸ We're part of God's family,
God's family, God's family
We're part of God's family,
His children we are! *(hold hands)*

❹ Let's spread the good news,
The good news, the good news.
Let's spread the good news,
The Savior has come! *(raise arms)*

☆ Let's Remember

Play this riddle-review game to help children remember God's people and promises. Say each riddle slowly. Provide more clues, if needed.

- I'm thinking about the first people God made and how he promised them a Savior through the family of their new son, Seth. *(Adam and Eve)*
- I'm thinking about a family God promised to save from a flood. *(Noah and his family)*
- I'm thinking of a man God promised would become a great nation. *(Abraham)*
- I'm thinking of a good king through whom God would send the promised Savior one day. *(David)*
- I'm thinking of someone who is the promised Savior. *(Jesus, God's Son)*

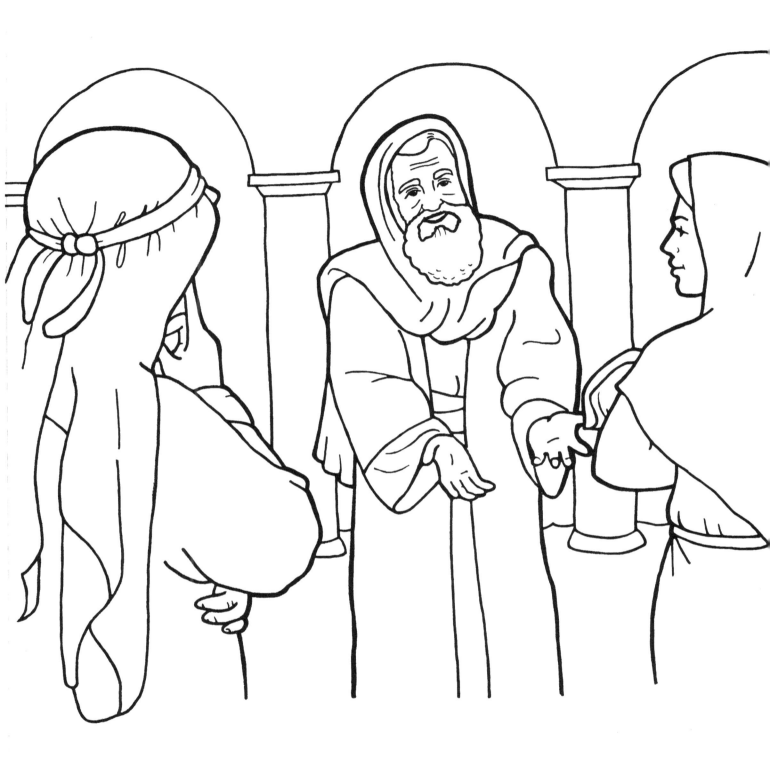

Simeon saw the Savior.

Luke 2:22–35

Simeon saw the Savior.
Luke 2:22–35

☆Let's Talk

SAY Simeon was an old man. God had promised Simeon that he would not die before he had seen the promised Savior. Simeon waited, believing that God would keep his promise. Then one day, the Holy Spirit led him to the temple.

ASK The picture shows Simeon at the temple. *What else do you see?*

SAY Mary and Joseph brought baby Jesus to the temple to present him to the Lord and to give a special offering.

ASK *How do you think Simeon felt when he saw baby Jesus?*

SAY Simeon joyfully took baby Jesus in his arms and praised God. He announced that Jesus was sent to save all God's people from their sins.

☆Let's Build

Tell your students that Mary and Joseph took baby Jesus to the temple, the place where God's people went to offer sacrifices and worship God. Today, God's people gather to worship him as a congregation in a church. Gather **wooden building blocks** and invite the children to build a temple or a church. Ask the children to name the structure they are going to build before they begin. And as they work, discuss how people would use the building they are making.

☆Let's Praise

Praise God for keeping his promise to send his Son to be the Savior.

SING "Come and Praise the Lord Our King." *Preschool Vol. 1* CD (track 7) Songbook, p. 12

LISTEN to songs about Jesus while coloring (tracks 7–12, *Preschool Vol. 1* CD).

SAY a prayer of praise, thanking God for loving us and for sending Jesus to be our Savior!

Wise men went to worship Jesus.

Matthew 2:1–23

 **Wise men went to worship Jesus.**
Matthew 2:1–23

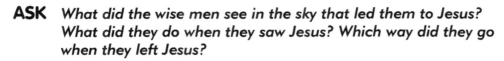

☆Let's Talk

ASK *What did the wise men see in the sky that led them to Jesus? What did they do when they saw Jesus? Which way did they go when they left Jesus?*

SAY God caused a bright star to guide the men to young Jesus, who lived in Bethlehem with Joseph and Mary. When the wise men saw the child, they bowed down and worshiped him. They gave him wonderful gifts of gold, sweet perfume, and spices. Then they went back to their own country by another way. God warned them not to return to King Herod in Jerusalem. The cruel king wanted to find out where Jesus was so he could harm the young child.

ASK *What was God's plan for his Son, Jesus?*

SAY God's plan was that Jesus would grow up and be the Savior of the world. Nothing could stop God's plan. God's power kept Jesus safe from an evil king!

☆Let's Pretend

Have the children copy your actions as you recall the story this way.

1. **First, the wise men went to Jerusalem and saw King Herod.** *(place open hands on either side of head as though wearing a crown)*
2. **Next, the star led them to the house in Bethlehem where Jesus lived.** *(draw large star shape with right index finger)*
3. **Then the wise men worshiped Jesus and gave him special gifts.** *(extend arms and hands, palms up)*
4. **Lastly, the wise men returned home another way.** *(turn around and walk across the room)*

☆Let's Make

Print the words **God cares for me** in the middle of a large sheet of **poster board**. Remind children that God kept Jesus safe from Herod. Talk about ways Jesus cares for them each day. He gives them families, homes, food, and clothing, and he keeps them safe. Give the children **paper** and **crayons** and have them draw and color one way God takes care of them. Cut out the pictures and **glue** them around the words on the sheet of poster board to make a border. Let the children tell what their pictures show.

Jesus went to the temple when he was 12 years old.
Luke 2:41–52

☆Let's Talk

ASK Jesus and his parents went on a long journey to celebrate Passover. *Where did they go?*

SAY They went to the temple in Jerusalem. Now that Jesus was 12 years old, he could attend temple services with Joseph and the other men for the first time.

ASK After celebrating Passover, Jesus was not with Mary and Joseph when they began the long trip home. *Where was he?*

SAY When Mary and Joseph found Jesus, he was in the temple sitting among the teachers of the law as they discussed God's Word. Jesus was asking and answering questions, and the teachers were amazed that he knew so much about God and the Scriptures. Even as a child, Jesus always pleased God!

☆Let's Travel

1. Pretend to go on a journey from Nazareth, the home of Jesus and his family, all the way to Jerusalem! Tape **masking tape** to the floor to make a long, winding trail.

2. Let the children line up at "Nazareth" at one end of the trail. At your signal, the first child walks with his or her feet on the tape, going all the way to "Jerusalem" at the other end. Children continue taking turns until each child in the line has had a turn.

3. Then children can take turns returning from Jerusalem to Nazareth. This time, they can choose to walk, hop, skip, or crawl back along the tape trail!

☆Let's Rhyme

Gather in a circle. Teach the children this action rhyme.

> **Jesus loved his Father in heaven,** *(point up)*
> **And pleased him every day.** *(cross hands over heart)*
> **He did what Mary and Joseph said—** *(point to a grown-up in the room)*
> **We, too, are called to obey!** *(join hands around the circle)*

Then talk about ways we can follow the example Jesus gave us. For example, we can know and learn God's Word to serve him, we can learn to obey God by obeying our parents and teachers, and so on.

John told about Jesus.

Matthew 3

John told about Jesus.
Matthew 3

☆Let's Talk

ASK *Who do you see in the picture?*

SAY John preached to the people by the Jordan River. He told the people they needed to be sorry for their sin, turn away from it, and get ready for the coming Savior. Many people believed John's message. They were sorry for their wrongdoing and were baptized.

ASK Jesus came along. *What did he ask John to do?*

SAY Jesus was baptized by John because he knew this was what God wanted him to do. Jesus had never sinned and did not need to repent. He had come to be the Savior of his people. It was time for his work of teaching and healing to begin!

ASK *What do you think happened after John baptized Jesus?*

SAY God spoke from heaven. He said, "This is my beloved Son, with whom I am well pleased." *(Matthew 3:17)*

☆Let's Sing and Move

Give each child a colorful **crepe-paper streamer** about 2 feet in length. Gather children in an open area. Play the song "Jesus Loves Even Me." Let the children move about the room waving their streamers as they sing along.

Preschool Vol. 1 CD

☆Let's Pray

Join hands and form a circle. Say this prayer together. You will say a few words, then the children will echo what you say.

> Dear God, I am sorry for my sin. Please forgive me for the wrong things that I do. Help me to trust and obey you. Help me to please you. Thank you for sending Jesus, my Savior. He came to earth to die for me so that my sins could be forgiven. Thank you for loving me! In Jesus' name, Amen.

Satan tempted Jesus 3 times.

Luke 4:1–13

 **Satan tempted Jesus 3 times.**
Luke 4:1–13

☆Let's Talk

SAY God led Jesus into the desert. Jesus stayed there for 40 days and nights.

SAY Jesus did not eat food during the day. Imagine how hungry and weak Jesus must have been. During that time, Satan tempted Jesus. He knew that Jesus had come to save God's people from sin and death, so Satan tried to get Jesus to disobey God and not do the work God had sent him to do.

ASK *Did Satan get Jesus to disobey God?*

SAY Satan failed to get Jesus to disobey God. Jesus used God's Word to say no to Satan. So the evil one went away and left Jesus alone for a time.

☆Let's Pretend

Gather the children in the center of the room. Tell them you are all going to take an imaginary trip in the desert. Children must look at what you do, listen to what you say, and copy your actions.

> **The desert is very hot and dry** *(fan yourself)*. **It's hard to walk around because it's so sandy and rocky** *(walk in place slowly)*. **There's a palm tree. Let's go sit under it and take a nap** *(walk to another place in the room, sit on the floor, and pretend to take a nap)*. **I think it's time to go home. Maybe those camels over there will give us a ride!** *(stretch, stand up, shade eyes as if looking off in the distance, then bounce up and down slowly as if riding a camel)*

☆Let's Give Thanks

Everyone sit in a circle. Begin by naming these things you are thankful to God for.

- I'm thankful that God loves us so much he sent Jesus to be our Savior.
- I'm thankful that Jesus forgives our sin.
- I'm thankful that he helps us say no to Satan.
- I'm thankful that he helps us to learn and obey his Word.

Then let each child take a turn and add on something for which he or she is thankful.

Luke 4

© GCP www.gcp.org
OK to photocopy for church and home use

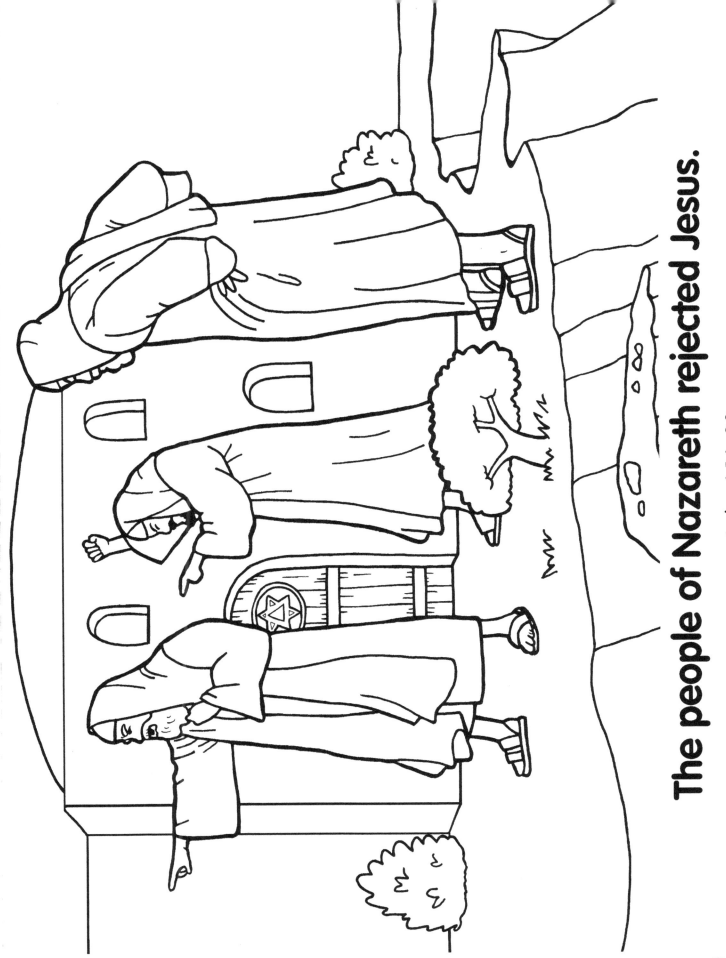

The people of Nazareth rejected Jesus.
Luke 4:14–30

☆Let's Talk

SAY Jesus went from town to town teaching God's Word and healing the sick. Then he went back to Nazareth, the town where he grew up. On the Sabbath day, Jesus went to the synagogue.

ASK *What happened when Jesus read from the Old Testament and said he was the Savior God had promised to send?*

SAY The people did not believe in Jesus. So he warned them, and they became very angry.

ASK *What does the picture show?*

SAY The people forced Jesus out of the synagogue and out of town. They would have thrown him off the edge of a cliff, but God protected Jesus and Jesus walked away unharmed.

☆Let's Sing and Do

To help the children think about Bible truths from the story of Jesus' visit to Nazareth, sing and do motions for the following song. Note that the children will need their **coloring pages**. Sing to the tune *Mary Had a Little Lamb*.

Preschool Vol. 2 CD

❶ Jesus went to Nazareth,
Nazareth, Nazareth.
Jesus went to Nazareth
to preach the Word of God.
(hold page out like a book)

❷ People there did not believe,
not believe, not believe.
People there did not believe
he was the promised One.
(peek around page, sadly)

❸ Jesus is our Savior,
our Savior, our Savior!
Jesus is our Savior.
It says so in God's Word.
(wave page around)

❹ He came for those who trust in him,
trust in him, trust in him.
He came for those who trust in him.
My heart belongs to God!
(hold page over heart)

Jesus called his first disciples.
Luke 5:1–11

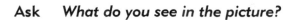

☆Let's Talk

Ask   *What do you see in the picture?*

Say   Jesus showed his power over nature by giving some fishermen a huge catch of fish. The men knew that this was a miracle. Only God could make so many fish in the lake swim into their nets. Jesus must be God!

Ask   *What did Jesus say to the men?*

Say   Jesus said that from now on they would catch men. Jesus told them to follow him. The fishermen left their boats, nets, and fish behind and followed Jesus!

☆Let's Move

Invite the children to walk slowly in a circle. Call out an action based on the Bible story. You can model the motions for the children to imitate while they walk.

1. **Clean your fishing nets.** *(rub your right hand back and forth over your open left palm)*
2. **Let down your nets in the water.** *(pretend to drop something to the side, using both hands)*
3. **Swim like fish.** *(put hands together and move them side to side in front of you)*
4. **Pull in your nets.** *(put arms out, close fingers, then pull them in)*
5. **Leave your nets and fish behind!** *(lead the children out of the circle and march around the room, single file)*

☆Let's Praise and Do

Cut out a bunch of simple fish shapes from **construction paper**. Use them to make steppingstones around the room. Let the children listen to and sing "Jesus Calls" as they take turns walking from one fish steppingstone to the next.

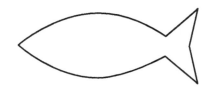

(track 10) *Preschool Vol. 1* CD
Songbook, p. 15

Jesus' first miracle: changing water into wine

John 2:1–11

Jesus' first miracle: changing water into wine
John 2:1–11

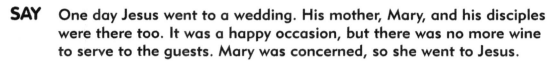

☆ Let's Talk and Wonder

SAY One day Jesus went to a wedding. His mother, Mary, and his disciples were there too. It was a happy occasion, but there was no more wine to serve to the guests. Mary was concerned, so she went to Jesus.

ASK *What did Mary think Jesus could do?*

SAY Mary was sure that Jesus could help. Jesus told his mother that only when the right time came would he show God's power.

ASK *What did Jesus do when the right time came?*

SAY Jesus told the servants to fill six large stone jars with water. When all the jars were filled, Jesus told the servants to pour some out and give it to the man in charge of the wedding. The man tasted the drink. It was very good wine. Jesus had changed the water into wine!

SAY I wonder what the disciples thought when they saw what Jesus did . . .

SAY When the disciples saw the miracle Jesus did, they began to understand that he had the power and greatness of God. Jesus showed them God's glory.

☆ Let's Make

1. Outline in large block letters **Jesus Is God** on a length of **shelf paper** to make a banner. Let children color the letters and decorate the banner with **glitter glue** and **praise stickers**.
2. While children work on the banner, talk some more about the miracle Jesus did and how he did miracles so that people would trust him as God. Explain that Jesus is God the Son, our powerful Savior who came to save us from our sins.
3. Hang the banner where everyone can see it!

☆ Let's Sing and Pray

Listen to "Jesus Revealed His Glory." Then have the children bow their heads as you lead them in this prayer.

Preschool Vol. 2 CD Songbook, p. 19

> Dear God, thank you that Jesus showed us your glory when he changed water into wine at the wedding. Thank you that he gave us a sign of your wonderful greatness that people could see. Thank you that he is God the Son, our powerful Savior. Please help me to trust in him. In Jesus' name, Amen.

Nicodemus visited Jesus at night.
John 3:1–21

☆ Let's Talk

ASK *What do you see in the picture?*

SAY Nicodemus, an important leader of the Jews, went to visit Jesus at night to learn more about him. Jesus told him that no one can enter the kingdom of God unless he is born again. Jesus explained to Nicodemus that he was not talking about being born as a tiny baby. He was talking about something different.

ASK *What does it mean to be born again?*

SAY Jesus explained that God loves us and sent his Son, Jesus, to die on the cross for our sins. God calls us to turn away from our sin and trust the Savior. The Holy Spirit works in our hearts, giving us faith in Jesus for forgiveness of sins and the gift of new life. That is what it means to be born again.

SAY What good news for Nicodemus and for us! Jesus loves us, saves us, and calls us his children!

☆ Let's Rhyme and Pretend

Let the children pretend to be Nicodemus visiting Jesus at night. As you say the rhyme, have them copy your actions.

> **Nicodemus tiptoes through town at night,** *(tiptoe in place)*
> **He visits Jesus—what a grand sight!** *(stand still, bow low to the ground)*
> **Nicodemus listens to all he hears,** *(sit down, cup face in hands)*
> **He's quite puzzled, but knows Jesus cares!** *(raise hands, palms up, shrug)*
>
> **Jesus tells him, "You must be born again,"** *(cross hands over heart)*
> **The Savior came to give new life to sinful men!** *(form cross with both arms)*
> **Nicodemus is glad for what Jesus said,** *(nod head, wide grin)*
> **Now it's time to go home and go to bed!** *(wave, turn around, tiptoe in place)*

☆ Let's Sing and Pray

Sing the first verse of "How Great Is the Love of the Father." Then pray this prayer.

 Preschool Vol. 2 CD Songbook, p. 14

> Dear Father, thank you for loving me. Thank you for saving me through your Son, Jesus. Thank you for making me your child. In Jesus' name, Amen.

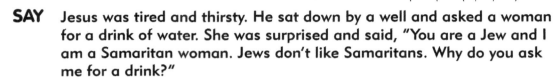

The woman at the well learned about living water from Jesus.
John 4:1–42

☆ Let's Talk

SAY Jesus was tired and thirsty. He sat down by a well and asked a woman for a drink of water. She was surprised and said, "You are a Jew and I am a Samaritan woman. Jews don't like Samaritans. Why do you ask me for a drink?"

SAY Jesus was kind to her. He offered her a wonderful gift. He said he could give her living water. Jesus was talking about life that lasts forever that only he could give. Jesus is the promised Savior who came to save sinners. Like every other person, the Samaritan woman was a sinner in need of a Savior!

ASK *What do you think the Samaritan woman did?*

SAY She left her water pot behind and hurried to the village to tell other people the good news about Jesus. The Samaritans hurried back to the well to see Jesus for themselves. Many listened to his teaching, repented of their sin, and trusted Jesus as their Savior!

☆ Let's Sing and Act

Sing and do these actions to the tune *Here We Go Round the Mulberry Bush*.

Preschool Vol. 2 CD

This is the way we go to the well,
(walk around, then gather at the "well")
Go to the well, go to the well.
This is the way we go to the well,
So early in the morning.

More verses:

This is the way we carry water
(pretend to carry a water pot)

This is the way we spread good news
(walk away from the well, then pretend to tell someone about the Savior)

This is the way we hurry back
(return quickly to the well as a group)

This is the way we thank the Savior
(fold hands in prayer)

☆ Let's Pray

Lead children in saying this prayer.

> Dear God, we are sinners in need of a Savior. Thank you that Jesus saves sinners. Help us to be sorry for our sin. Help us to trust Jesus and receive from him the gift of life that lasts forever. In Jesus' name, Amen.

Love your enemies and pray for them.

Matthew 5:43–48

Love your enemies and pray for them.
Matthew 5:43–48

☆Let's Talk and Wonder

SAY A large crowd of people gathered on the mountainside to see and hear Jesus. The disciples sat beside Jesus. They listened carefully as he taught them how God's people should live. He told them to love and pray for their enemies.

ASK *What did Jesus mean when he said that God's people should love and pray for their enemies?*

SAY Jesus was telling his followers to love everyone—even people who don't love God and don't love them back. He was telling his followers to pray for those who hate them.

SAY I wonder what the disciples thought when they heard what Jesus said . . .

SAY The disciples and all God's children were once God's enemies. But God loved them and sent his Son to be their Savior. Now God's people are no longer God's enemies. We are children of God and are commanded to love the way God loves. That means loving those who don't love Jesus and who don't love us. We need God's help to forgive our enemies, pray for them, and show kindness to them!

☆Let's Play

Play this active game to remind children that Jesus wants us to show that we love our enemies by what we say and do. Sit in a circle. Give a **red, green, or blue paper strip** to each child. Tell the children to listen as you call out a color, give a command, and do an action. Each child holding a paper strip of the color you named stands up, repeats the command, and imitates your action. Have everyone sit down. Then move on to the next color, command, and action. Play until all commands have been given.

Red I'll pray for those who are mean to me. *(fold hands in prayer)*
Green I'll walk away when a bully tries to pick a fight. *(turn around, walk away)*
Blue I'll say "Hi" to someone who ignores me. *(high-five someone)*
Red I'll share my toys with those who won't share with me. *(hold out hands, palms facing up)*
Green I'll smile at those who make fun of me. *(draw a smile on your face with your fingers)*
Blue I'll forgive my enemy. *(form a cross with both arms)*

☆Let's Pray

Dear God, we pray for our enemies. Help us to love and forgive them, just as you do. In Jesus' name, Amen.

**Good trees bear good fruit.
Bad trees bear bad fruit.**

Matthew 7:16–20

**Good trees bear good fruit.
Bad trees bear bad fruit.**
Matthew 7:16–20

☆Let's Talk and Wonder

SAY One day, Jesus told his disciples about a tree and its fruit. Good trees give good fruit. Bad trees make bad fruit. Looking at the fruit tells you what kind of tree it came from. A fruit tree always makes the same kind of fruit.

ASK Look at the picture. *What do you see?*

SAY An apple tree always bears apples.

ASK *Why do you think Jesus told his disciples about trees and fruit?*

SAY Just like good fruit from a good tree, God's children say and do good things because they belong to their heavenly Father, who is perfectly good. God's children need to depend on him to help them trust Jesus and obey his teachings. We need God the Holy Spirit to make good fruit grow in our hearts!

SAY I wonder what others think when they see that we are trusting and obeying Jesus . . .

SAY When we say and do things that please God, we show others the love of Jesus. We show that God is helping us grow more and more like Jesus!

☆Let's Make

1. Print **God makes us more like Jesus** in the middle of a large sheet of **poster board**. Bring in **pictures of a variety of good fruit**. Let children **glue** the pictures around the caption.

2. Talk about ways God makes us more like Jesus. Under each fruit, print one way we can be "fruitful" members of God's family. For example, under a strawberry you might print, "God helps me love others"; under a banana, "God helps me to be kind"; and so on.

☆Let's Sing

Sing this active rhyme to the tune *The Farmer in the Dell*. *Preschool Vol. 2* CD

My Father makes me grow, *(crouch down, then stand up tall)*
Like Jesus every day. *(point up)*
I'll say and do what pleases him, *(cup hands around mouth, cross hands over heart)*
I'll trust him and obey! *(fold hands in prayer, then open them to make a Bible)*

Matthew 7

© GCP www.gcp.org
OK to photocopy for church and home use

The wise man built his house on a rock.

Matthew 7:24–27

The wise man built his house on a rock.
Matthew 7:24–27

☆ Let's Talk

ASK Look at the picture. *What do you see?*

SAY Jesus told a story about a wise man and a foolish man. The wise man built his house on solid rock. When a storm came, it rained hard and the winds blew and beat against the house. But the house did not fall. It stood strong and safe because it was built on rock.

ASK *What do you think the foolish man did?*

SAY The foolish man built his house on sand. Soon a storm came and rain poured down. The water washed the sand away and the winds blew against the house. The house fell with a loud crash!

ASK *Why did Jesus tell his followers this story?*

SAY Jesus said that everyone who hears his words and puts them into practice is like a wise man who builds his house on a rock. We have the Bible to tell us how Jesus wants his children to live. If we know what Jesus says and we do it, we are like the wise man. But if we know what Jesus says and decide not to believe and obey him, we are like the foolish man instead. God wants us to trust him and obey his Word every day!

☆ Let's Play

1. This game is a variation of *Red Light, Green Light*. You will be the leader and stand at one end of the room, holding your **Bible**. Have children stand on the opposite side of the room. Hold up your Bible, say **"Obey God's Word,"** and turn your back to the group. While your back is turned, children will walk toward you. When you turn and face them, they must stop. If you see anyone still moving, that child must go back to the starting point.

2. The child who reaches you first tells something Jesus said or did that we should remember and put into practice, or names a favorite Bible story. He or she also gets to be the leader for the next round!

☆ Let's Pray

Invite children to bow their heads and close their eyes. Lead them in saying this prayer.

Dear God, thank you for your Word. Help me to become wise by hearing and obeying your Word. In Jesus' name, Amen.

Peter said Jesus is the Christ, the Son of the living God.
Matthew 16:13–18

☆ Let's Talk and Wonder

SAY Jesus had been teaching his disciples. He asked them a very important question. "Who do you say I am?" Jesus asked.

ASK I wonder what the disciples did when Jesus asked them that question. *What does the picture show?*

SAY The Bible tells us that Peter answered by saying, "You are the Christ, the Son of the living God."

ASK *How did Peter know this?*

SAY God made Peter know that Jesus is God's Son. Jesus went on to explain that he is the promised Messiah and King who was sent down to earth from heaven to suffer and die for the sins of his people. Peter could not figure this out for himself and neither could the other disciples.

☆ Let's Make

1 Print *"You are the Christ, the Son of the living God"* in large block letters on **poster board**. Open your **Bible** to Matthew 16:16 and point to the words as you tell the children that what Peter said is found in the Bible. Remind them that we can thank God for his Word, which tells us about the Savior.

2 Set out **crayons** and **markers** so that children can color in the letters. Then provide some items to **glue** onto the letters: **glitter glue, rice, beans, cotton balls, popped popcorn,** and so on. When they are finished working, mount the poster on a bulletin board and say the words together.

☆ Let's Rhyme

Everyone sit in a circle. Teach the children the following rhyme and have them clap as they say the words rhythmically. Emphasize the syllables that are capitalized.

1 WE have HEARD
FROM God's WORD—
JEsus IS the SAvior!

2 HE'S God's SON
HE'S the ONE—
SENT to BE our SAvior!

3 GOD helps ME
So I can SEE—
JEsus IS my SAvior!

 **Jesus revealed his glory.**
Matthew 17:1–8

☆Let's Listen and Talk

Gather the children together and read aloud the story of the Transfiguration found in Matthew 17:1–8.

ASK *What do you see in the picture?*

SAY The disciples saw the wonderful, bright glory of Jesus.

ASK *What did the disciples hear when the cloud appeared and covered them?*

SAY They heard God's voice from heaven. He told them to listen to Jesus, his Son whom he loved.

ASK *How can we find out what Jesus says?*

SAY We can find out what Jesus says to his people in the Bible. He speaks to us through God's Word, telling us how to please him by living trusting and obedient lives, and by confessing our sin when we disobey.

☆Let's Pretend and Sing

❶ Lead the children on a pretend walk up a mountain. Remind them that they are using their *feet* to climb along the path. At the top, ask the children to use their *eyes* to look around. Tell them to use their *ears* to listen for sounds. Show them how to use their *hands* to shade their eyes from the bright sunlight.

❷ Tell them they are going to listen to and sing a song about using their whole bodies to serve God! Lead them in singing "Two Little Eyes."  *Preschool Vol. 1* CD Songbook, p. 16

☆Let's Pray

Gather the children around you. Invite them to say this prayer after you, phrase by phrase.

> **Dear God, thank you for sending Jesus to be the promised Savior. Thank you for giving us your Word so we can find out what Jesus says to us. Give us hearts that trust and obey him. Help us use our eyes, ears, feet, and hands to serve him! In Jesus' name, Amen.**

The king forgave his servant who owed him a lot of money.
Matthew 18:21–35

☆ Let's Talk

ASK Jesus told a story about a king whose servant owed him a lot of money. *What do you see in the picture?*

SAY The servant went to the king and told him he was sorry he could not pay it back right away. The king forgave the servant. He told the servant he didn't have to pay what he owed and let him go. The servant left the king and visited a man who owed him a little money.

ASK *What do you think the servant did to the man?*

SAY The servant demanded his money. When the man couldn't pay, the servant did not forgive him. He threw the man in jail. When the king heard what the servant did, he called him in. "You wicked servant," the king said. "You should have forgiven the man, just as I forgave you!" Then the king sent the servant to jail.

ASK *Why do you think Jesus told this story?*

SAY Jesus told this story to teach God's people that they should forgive others from the heart, just as Jesus has forgiven them.

☆ Let's Trace

Print the word *Forgive* in dotted lines on a sheet of **paper**. Make **photocopies** and let children use a **crayon, marker,** or **pencil** to trace the letters. As children work, talk about ways to show forgiveness to others.

☆ Let's Act

Set out a **toy crown, bathrobes,** and **sandals** to be used as props as you review the story Jesus told about forgiveness. Let children put on costumes and act out the parts of the king, the servant, and the man thrown in jail as you retell the story.

☆ Let's Sing a Prayer

Sing this prayer to the tune "Part of the Family of God." *Preschool Vol. 2* CD (track 27)

> Forgive one another each day,
> Dear God, please help us, we pray.
> You've forgiven our wrong; to you we belong!
> Forgive one another each day!

Conclude by saying **In Jesus' name, Amen.**

The rich young man and poor widow

Matthew 19:16–30; Luke 21:1–3

The rich young man and poor widow
Matthew 19:16–30; Luke 21:1–3 (Mark 10:17–27; Exodus 20:3)

☆ Let's Talk

ASK *Who do you see in the picture?*

SAY A rich young man went to see Jesus. But he was not ready to follow him. The man loved the things God had given him more than he loved Jesus, and he loved himself more than others. Sadly, he walked away from Jesus.

SAY After Jesus spoke to him, I wonder if the rich young man realized that he didn't really love or trust God . . .

SAY Another time, a poor widow put two small coins in the money box at the temple. It was not very much, but it was all she had to offer God. Jesus saw what she did and said she gave more than anyone else because she gave everything. The poor widow showed that she loved God more than the things he had given her. Jesus wants his children to love him more than any of his gifts to us. He wants us to love him best!

☆ Let's Feel and Share

1 Gather the following objects: **apple, package of cookies, coins, board game, book, crayon box, ball.** Secretly place one of the objects inside a **bag.** Have a child put his hand inside the bag, feel the object, and guess what it is without looking. When the correct guess is given, remove the object from the bag. Talk about ways to share it with others.

2 Continue with the remaining objects. Make sure everyone has a turn. Point out that Jesus wants us to love him first and best. He wants us to trust him to give us what we need, and he wants us to share what we have with others.

3 Afterward, share the cookies as a snack. (Be aware of allergies.)

☆ Let's Sing and Pray

Sing this prayer to the tune *The Farmer in the Dell*.

Preschool Vol. 2 CD, track 45

> Thank you for saving me,
> Your child I'll always be.
> Help me love you most of all,
> Dear God, on you I'll call.

Conclude the prayer by saying **In Jesus' name, Amen.**

Matthew 19; Luke 21

© GCP www.gcp.org
OK to photocopy for church and home use

Jesus calmed the storm.
Mark 4:35–41

☆Let's Talk

SAY Jesus and his disciples got in a boat and pushed off from the land to go to the other side of the lake. Jesus fell asleep in the back of the boat. Suddenly, the skies were filled with dark clouds.

ASK *What do you think happened next?*

SAY A storm came. The wind blew hard, the waves grew large, and the boat rocked from side to side. The disciples were frightened because they thought the boat would sink. Jesus was still fast asleep. "Teacher," they cried, "don't you care if we drown?"

ASK *What did Jesus do?*

SAY Jesus told the wind and the waves to be still. When he made the storm go away, the disciples said to each other, "Who is this? Even the winds and waves obey him."

ASK *What did Jesus show by calming the storm?*

SAY Jesus showed that he is Lord over creation and that he is God. He had come to earth to be the Savior of the world. The One who came to save his people from their sins could quickly calm a scary storm!

☆Let's Play

Sit in **chairs** in a large circle to play *Storm on the Lake*. Select one child to be the caller in the center of the circle. The caller says **"Rock to this** (or 'that') **side"** and points in the direction that children must move. Then children move the next seat over in the direction that is indicated. Play continues as children in their pretend boats are directed to rock right or left. From time to time, whoever is in the center should call out **"Storm on the lake!"** At this point all children, including the caller, should get up and find a new seat anywhere in the circle. The child left without a seat becomes the new caller.

☆Let's Share and Pray

1. Talk about times when your children may be afraid. Encourage them to turn to Jesus for help. Remind them that Jesus is our powerful and loving Savior. He is with us and will always take care of us.

2. Lead them in saying this prayer: **Dear Jesus, thank you that you are God and that you have power over everything. Thank you that you are my Savior. I'm glad that you are always with me. You take care of me and protect me. Help me to trust you always, especially when I'm afraid. In your name I pray, Amen.**

Jesus raised Jairus's daughter from the dead.

Mark 5:21–43

Jesus raised Jairus's daughter from the dead.
Mark 5:21–43

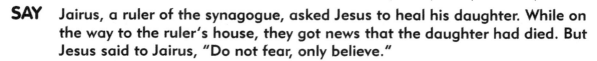

☆ Let's Talk

SAY Jairus, a ruler of the synagogue, asked Jesus to heal his daughter. While on the way to the ruler's house, they got news that the daughter had died. But Jesus said to Jairus, "Do not fear, only believe."

ASK *Why did Jesus say these words to Jairus?*

SAY Jesus was teaching Jairus to trust him. When they got to the ruler's house, people were crying because the young girl was dead. When Jesus told them not to cry, they laughed at Jesus.

ASK *Why did they laugh?*

SAY Those people didn't know that Jesus is God and that he has power over death. Jesus told them to leave. Then he went over to where the young girl lay. Jesus held her hand and told her to get up. At his words, she became alive again.

ASK *How do you think Jairus and his wife felt when their daughter came back to life?*

SAY Jairus and his wife were very glad to see their daughter alive and well again. Jairus had come to Jesus for help and Jesus had helped him in a way that only God could. Jesus made Jairus's daughter live again. Jesus is the Lord of life!

☆ Let's Make

Print *Jesus came to save and help us* on a sheet of **paper**. Make a **photocopy** for each child. Let children draw and color pictures of themselves and their families under the caption. As they work, emphasize that all who believe in Jesus belong to him always. He cares for us and helps us each day. When he comes back again, all who trust in Jesus the Savior will live with him forever. There will be no more sickness, no more sadness, and no more death!

☆ Let's Listen and Sign

Listen to "I Belong to Jesus." Lead the children in signing key words.  *Preschool Vol. 2 CD*

1 I

2 belong

3 Jesus

Sign illustrations from *The Joy of Signing* © 1987 Gospel Publishing House

© GCP www.gcp.org
OK to photocopy for church and home use

Jesus fed 5,000 people with only 5 loaves and 2 fish.
Mark 6:30–44

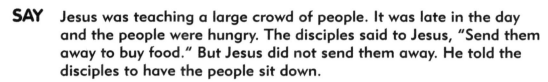

☆Let's Talk

SAY Jesus was teaching a large crowd of people. It was late in the day and the people were hungry. The disciples said to Jesus, "Send them away to buy food." But Jesus did not send them away. He told the disciples to have the people sit down.

ASK *When the people were seated, what did Jesus do?*

SAY A boy gave Jesus five barley loaves and two fish. Jesus thanked God for the food. Then Jesus started giving the food to the people. The five loaves and two fish became more and more, enough to feed every person in that large crowd. And there were enough leftovers to fill 12 baskets!

ASK *How did Jesus show his love and care for the people that day?*

SAY Jesus showed his love and care by teaching the people God's Word and by feeding them all when they were hungry. Jesus was showing that he is God, because only God could do this miracle.

☆Let's Eat and Say

Weather permitting, have a picnic outdoors. (Children may just as happily have their picnic indoors.) Set out a large **blanket or quilt** for children to sit on. Serve **fish-shaped crackers, fruit,** and a **drink**. As children eat and drink, mention some of the ways Jesus showed love and care for his disciples and others around him. He turned water into wine, he calmed a storm, he taught people about God, and he fed 5,000. Most important of all, he died on the cross for the sins of his people!

☆Let's Make and Praise

Make praise tambourines. Give each child **two paper plates**. Color the bottom sides of the plates. Then place a handful of **dried beans** in one plate, cover it with the second plate, and fasten the edges with **tape**. Add colorful **ribbon or paper streamers**.

Children can shake their tambourines as you lead them in singing this praise song to the tune *Mary Had a Little Lamb*.

 *Preschool Vol. 2* CD

❶ Jesus is my Savior,
My Savior, my Savior.
Jesus is my Savior,
I'll praise him every day!

❷ He provides for all my needs,
All my needs, all my needs.
He provides for all my needs,
He's so good to me!

Mark 6

© GCP www.gcp.org
OK to photocopy for church and home use

Parents brought their children to Jesus.
Mark 10:13–16

☆ Let's Talk

ASK *What do you see in the picture? What else?*

SAY Jesus gladly welcomed little children and babies and took them in his arms. He put his hands on the children and blessed them and prayed for them. Then Jesus talked to the parents and the disciples. He told them they needed to receive the kingdom of God just like these little ones.

ASK *Why did the children and grown-ups need Jesus?*

SAY They were helpless without him. They needed what only Jesus could give. Everyone needs Jesus. Jesus is the Savior who loves us and came to die for us, young and old alike. We are all helpless without him and we need him to teach us how to trust him completely.

☆ Let's Listen and Use Our Hands

Let the children listen to "Jesus Loves Me" while you lead them in some sign language to emphasize key words of the song.

 *Preschool Vol. 1* CD

1 Jesus

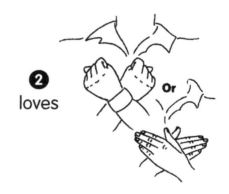
2 loves

3 Bible

4 belong

Sign Illustrations from *The Joy of Signing*
© 1987 Gospel Publishing House

Mark 10

© GCP www.gcp.org
OK to photocopy for church and home use

Jesus healed blind Bartimaeus.

Mark 10:46–52

Jesus healed blind Bartimaeus.
Mark 10:46–52

☆ Let's Talk

ASK *What do you see in the picture?*

SAY When Jesus was passing by, a blind man named Bartimaeus shouted, "Jesus, Son of David, have mercy on me!" People told Bartimaeus to be quiet, but he shouted still louder. He had faith that the Savior could help him.

ASK *What do you think Jesus did?*

SAY Jesus did a miracle. He said to Bartimaeus, "Go your way; your faith has made you well."

ASK *Why did Jesus heal Bartimaeus?*

SAY Jesus showed love and concern for Bartimaeus, who cried out to him in faith. Jesus did miracles so that people would trust him as God, their Savior.

ASK *What do you think Bartimaeus did when Jesus healed him?*

SAY Bartimaeus was very glad he could see. He followed Jesus along the road, praising God as he went. All the people who saw the miracle Jesus did praised God too.

☆ Let's Make

1. Give each child two circles of **construction paper**. Fold one circle in half.
2. **Glue** the bottom half to the lower half of the other circle.
3. Draw Bartimaeus's sad face on the circle folded and Bartimaeus's happy face on the open circle. Point out that Bartimaeus was sad at first when he was suffering. Then Bartimaeus was happy when Jesus healed him. Jesus cared for Bartimaeus, and Jesus cares for us!

☆ Let's Sing and Pray

1. Sing "Jesus Loves Me, This I Know." *Toddler Sing-Along With Me* CD (track 8)
2. Have the children bow their heads, close their eyes, and listen as you pray this prayer.

   Dear Jesus, we need you every day. Thank you for loving us and taking care of us. Help us to follow you gladly. We praise you for being our Savior. In your name we pray, Amen.

Mark 10

© GCP www.gcp.org
OK to photocopy for church and home use

Jesus healed a paralyzed man.

Luke 5:17–26

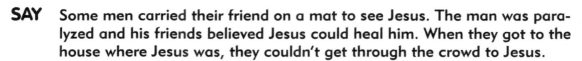

Jesus healed a paralyzed man.
Luke 5:17–26

☆Let's Talk and Wonder

SAY Some men carried their friend on a mat to see Jesus. The man was paralyzed and his friends believed Jesus could heal him. When they got to the house where Jesus was, they couldn't get through the crowd to Jesus.

ASK *What do you think the men did?*

SAY The men carried their friend up the stairs to the roof. They made a hole in the roof and lowered the man through the hole until he was right in front of Jesus.

ASK *What did Jesus do?*

SAY Jesus saw that the men trusted him. Jesus showed his authority as God when he forgave the paralyzed man's sins and then healed him. The man went home praising God and the people praised God too.

SAY I wonder if many people who saw Jesus heal the paralyzed man trusted him as God their Savior that day . . .

☆Let's Make

Give children a **half sheet of paper** each and let them draw pictures of times when they were sick or hurt. Let them **glue** their pictures on a large sheet of **poster board** with these words across the top: *Jesus my Savior takes care of me!* Talk about their pictures. Remind them that Jesus knows when we are sick, he hears our prayers, and he is the one who heals. We can trust him to take care of us.

☆Let's Pray

Lead the children in this responsive prayer. You will speak first and they are to listen to your words. When you stop speaking, they will say, "Thank you, dear Jesus."

Leader: **Lord Jesus, you came to earth to be our Savior.**
Children: Thank you, dear Jesus.
Leader: **You showed your love by living and dying for us.**
Children: Thank you, dear Jesus.
Leader: **You have the power and right to forgive sins and heal sickness.**
Children: Thank you, dear Jesus.
Leader: **Please forgive us when we sin.**
Children: Thank you, dear Jesus.
Leader: **We pray in your name.**
All: Amen.

A soldier's servant was healed by Jesus.

Luke 7:1–10

A soldier's servant was healed by Jesus.
Luke 7:1–10

☆ Let's Talk and Wonder

SAY Once there was an important soldier, called a centurion, who had a sick servant. He sent the leaders of the Jews to Jesus for help.

SAY I wonder what the centurion thought Jesus could do . . .

SAY The Jewish leaders found Jesus and asked him if he would heal the centurion's servant. So Jesus went with the men. When they were on their way to the centurion's house, his friends ran to meet Jesus with a message from the centurion. He had faith that Jesus could just say the word and his servant would be healed. Jesus didn't have to travel all the way to his house.

SAY Jesus told everyone he was amazed that the centurion had such great faith. When the centurion's friends hurried back to the house, they found that the sick servant had been made well. Jesus had healed him, just as the centurion knew he could!

☆ Let's Do

1. Use **colorful markers** to print the letters **F-A-I-T-H** on **large index cards**, one letter per card. Go over the word with the children. Explain that Jesus gives us faith. It is a gift God gives us so we can reach out and receive what Jesus did for us when he died on the cross to save us.

2. Sit on the floor in a circle. Place the cards in the middle of the circle. Ask the children to say the letters with you and then say the word *faith*. Tell children to close their eyes. Remove one index card. Ask which letter is missing. After they identify it, return the card and continue playing the game, removing a different letter each time. At the end of the activity, talk about the miracle Jesus did and how the centurion put his faith in Jesus.

☆ Let's Make and Sing

1. Make mini praise signs. Cut out a **heart shape** for each child. Write on each heart *Jesus is God my Savior.* Let children personalize their hearts with drawings and **stickers**. Cut two lines inside each heart. Slide a **drinking straw** through each heart.

2. Let children wave their mini praise signs as they sing "There Is Power in the Name of Jesus."

Preschool Vol. 2 CD
Songbook, p. 20

Jesus raised a widow's son to life.

Luke 7:11–17

Jesus raised a widow's son to life.
Luke 7:11–17

☆Let's Talk and Wonder

SAY When Jesus and his disciples came near the town of Nain, they saw a funeral. A widow's only son had died.

ASK *What do you think Jesus did?*

SAY Jesus comforted the widow. Then he raised her son back to life!

ASK *What do you see in the picture?*

SAY The young son sat up and began to talk. The mother was very glad to have her son alive again! All the people who saw what Jesus did were amazed. "God has come to help his people," they said and began praising him. Soon the good news about Jesus and his power over death spread throughout all the towns and cities!

☆Let's Sing and Move

Lead the children in singing the following active song to the tune *London Bridge Is Falling Down*.

 *Preschool Vol. 2* CD

① Aren't you glad to be alive?
Shake your fingers in the sky.
Aren't you glad to be alive?
Stretch your arms. Reach up high!

② Aren't you glad to be alive?
Make your feet go in the air.
Aren't you glad to be alive?
Shake your head. Pull your ear!

③ Aren't you glad to be alive?
Hug a friend and neighbor, too.
Aren't you glad to be alive?
Thank you, God; we praise you!

☆Let's Spread the Good News

Play *Telephone*. Sit in a circle. Whisper **"Jesus came to save his people"** to the first child. He whispers what he heard to the next child. Continue in this way until the message reaches the last child, who calls out what she heard. Repeat the activity more than once, whispering a different sentence about Jesus each time.

The forgiven woman believed Jesus.

Luke 7:36–50

The forgiven woman believed Jesus.
Luke 7:36–50

☆Let's Talk

SAY Jesus was having dinner at the home of Simon the Pharisee. A woman entered the room. She honored Jesus by rubbing his feet with perfumed ointment and wiping them with her hair.

ASK *What did Simon think when he saw what the woman did?*

SAY Simon thought, "If Jesus really came from God, he would know that this woman is a terrible sinner. He should know better than to let her touch him." Jesus knew what Simon was thinking.

ASK *What did Jesus say?*

SAY The sinful woman had come to Jesus to show her love and thankfulness. Simon had not invited Jesus to his house because he wanted to honor him. Unlike Simon, the woman came knowing how much she needed the Savior. Jesus turned to the woman and said, "Your sins are forgiven. . . . Your faith has saved you; go in peace."

☆Let's Make

Print *I love Jesus my Savior!* on a sheet of **paper**. Make a **photocopy** for each child. Let the children color the words. Then mount each page on colorful **construction paper**. Encourage the children to add borders made of hearts, **glitter glue**, or **praise stickers**. Suggest that children hang the poster at home.

☆Let's Pray

Lead the children in a responsive prayer. Explain that when you speak they must listen to your words. When you stop speaking, they are to say, "I love you, dear Jesus." At the end, everyone will say "Amen."

Leader: Dear Jesus, thank you for dying on the cross for my sin.
Children: I love you, dear Jesus.
Leader: Please forgive me.
Children: I love you, dear Jesus.
Leader: Thank you for your great love and forgiveness.
Children: I love you, dear Jesus.
Leader: Help me to grow in trusting and obeying you.
Children: I love you, dear Jesus.
Leader: We pray in Jesus' name.
All: Amen.

Jesus sent out his 12 disciples.
Luke 9:1–6

☆Let's Talk

ASK *Who are the men in the picture? Let's count them. How many are there?*

SAY Jesus chose 12 men to follow him as his disciples. That means they were followers of Jesus and learned from him. They were called to trust and obey him.

ASK *What special job did Jesus give his 12 disciples to do?*

SAY Jesus told them to go out and tell people about the Savior and the coming of God's kingdom. He told them to heal the sick and drive out demons.

ASK *Who gave the disciples the power to serve God?*

SAY Jesus, God's Son, gave them the power to be his disciples. He gave them everything they needed to trust and obey him.

☆Let's Cut, Paste, and Plan

❶ **Tape** a large sheet of **paper** to the wall or bulletin board. Print **Tell others about the Savior** across the top. Remind your children that if we belong to Jesus, we will want to tell others about the Savior, just as the disciples did.

❷ Set out age-appropriate **family magazines, glue sticks,** and **scissors.** Have the children look through the magazines and help them tear or cut out pictures of the kind of people they see during the week (for example, the postal carrier, T-ball coach, librarian, friends, and neighbors). Glue the pictures on the paper.

❸ As you discuss the mural, talk about ways to share the love of Jesus with the people your children interact with.

☆Let's Listen and Number

Get **12 sheets of paper.** Print numbers 1–12 on them, one number per sheet. Have the children stand in a line. Remind the children that Jesus called and sent out 12 disciples. Lead them in taking turns to place the numbered sheets in order on the floor from 1 to 12 as they listen to "Jesus Calls."

Preschool Vol. 1 CD

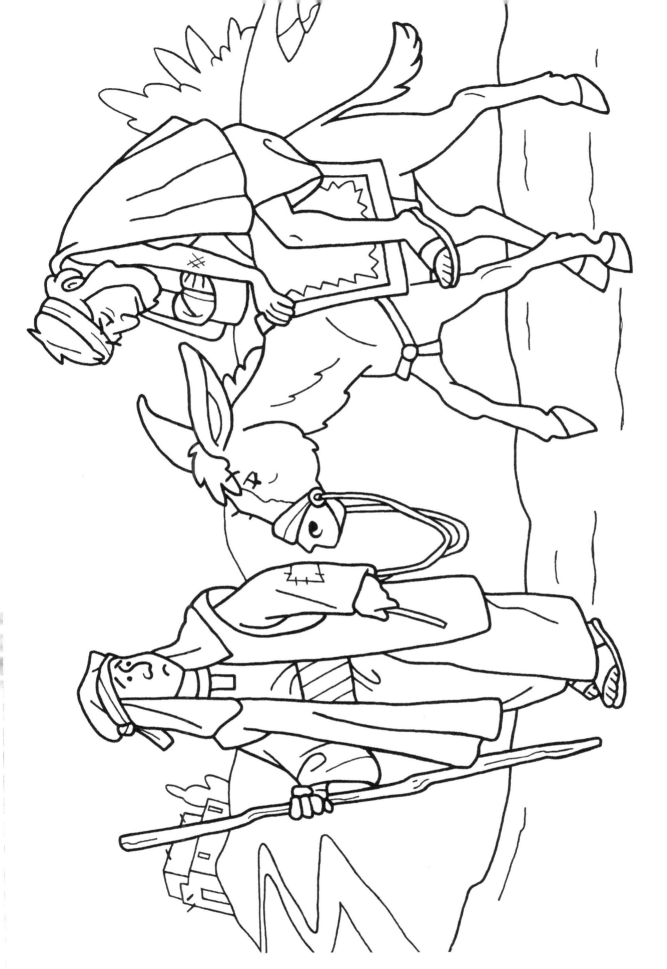

The good Samaritan helped the hurt man.
Luke 10:25–37

The good Samaritan helped the hurt man.
Luke 10:25–37

☆ Let's Talk

SAY Jesus told a story. He said that one day a man was walking down the road. A gang of bad men beat him up and robbed him. They took what he had and left him to die. A priest came along, but he would not help. He walked by on the other side of the road. Then another Jewish leader came by. He, too, passed by. Then a Samaritan man came along. At the time, Jews thought they were better than the Samaritans.

ASK *What do you see in the picture?*

SAY The Samaritan helped the hurt man by bandaging his wounds and giving him medicine. Then the Samaritan put him on his own donkey and took him to a place where he could rest and get well.

ASK *Why do you think Jesus told this story?*

SAY Jesus told this story to answer the question, Who is my neighbor? Jesus taught that each person God puts in our life is our neighbor. The Samaritan showed the love of a neighbor to a man who needed help. When we love and trust God, we will love and want to help others too.

☆ Let's Do

Use a **hole puncher** to punch holes around the edges of pieces of **tagboard,** one per child. Have everyone draw and color a picture of a kind thing he or she can do to be a good neighbor to someone. Then provide colorful lengths of **yarn** to thread through the holes.

☆ Let's Sing a Prayer

Lead children in singing this prayer to the tune *Twinkle, Twinkle Little Star*. Sing one line at a time and have them repeat it after you.

> Help me love You most of all,
> And help me love all others, too.
> Help me show love every day,
> In what I say and what I do.
> Help me love You most of all,
> Dear Father, all these things I pray.

Conclude the prayer by saying **In Jesus' name, Amen.**

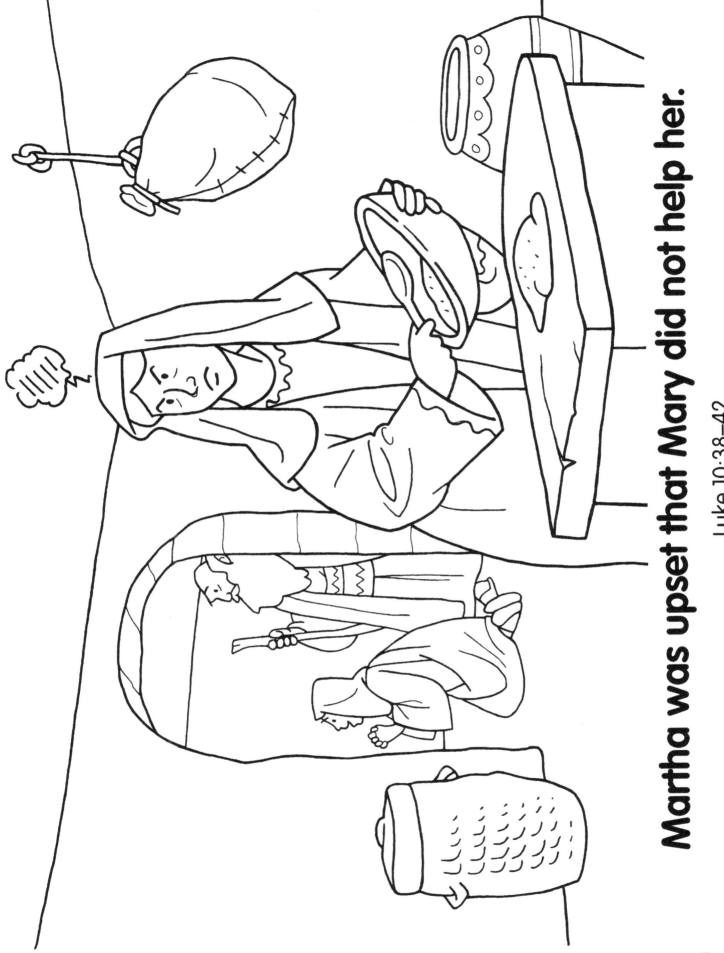

 # Martha was upset that Mary did not help her.
Luke 10:38–42

☆Let's Talk

ASK Look at the picture. *What do you see?*

SAY Jesus was at the home of Mary and Martha. Mary sat down on the floor next to Jesus. She wanted to listen to all the wonderful things that Jesus had to say. Martha was busy getting dinner ready.

ASK *What are some things Martha probably had to do to get ready?*

SAY Martha probably had to bake bread, cook meat, and wash vegetables. How would she get it all done? Martha started getting upset. She needed help!

ASK *What do you think Martha did?*

SAY Martha went to Jesus. "Lord, don't you care that my sister has left me to do the work by myself? Tell her to help me!" Martha said. Jesus replied that Martha was worried and upset about many things. Jesus went on to say that Mary had chosen the one thing that is needed. Mary had chosen to listen and learn from Jesus, and that it would never be taken away from her!

☆Let's Listen

1. Sit in a circle on the floor. Have the children cover their eyes with their hands. Tell them to listen carefully to the sounds you make. One at a time, make easy-to-recognize noises and let the children guess what they are. For example, crumple a sheet of paper, bounce a ball, ring a bell, shut a door, whistle a tune, and so on.

2. Let the children open their eyes. *Say* **We use our ears to hear all kinds of sounds.** *Hold up your Bible.* **We also use our ears to listen to God's Word, the Bible. We don't actually hear God speaking in our ears from heaven, but we do hear his words when someone reads the Bible to us and teaches us what it says.**

☆Let's Name Something

Gather the children around you. Hand your **Bible** to a child and name one thing you've learned about Jesus from God's Word. Then have the child hand the Bible to someone else and name something he has learned. Continue so everyone has a chance to name something. Examples: *I have learned that* . . . Jesus is our Savior; loves me; healed the sick; fed the people; stopped the storm; welcomed little children; died on the cross; rose from the dead; and so on.

The disciples asked Jesus to teach them how to pray.

Luke 11:1–4; Matthew 6:9–14

The disciples asked Jesus to teach them how to pray.
Luke 11:1–4; Matthew 6:9–14

☆Let's Talk and Wonder

SAY When Jesus lived on earth, he often went off by himself and prayed to his Father in heaven. The disciples noticed and asked Jesus to teach them to pray.

ASK *Why did they ask Jesus to teach them to pray?*

SAY The disciples wanted to know what kinds of things to pray to God, who was their Father in heaven, too.

ASK *What are some things Jesus taught in the prayer he gave his followers, known as the Lord's Prayer?*

SAY Jesus taught that when we pray we should praise God, ask for forgiveness, and ask for the things we need. God is pleased when his children come before him and tell him all the things that concern us, ask for his help, and praise and thank him.

☆Let's Listen

Slowly say or read the Lord's Prayer, found in Matthew 6:9–14, as the children listen.

☆Let's Sing

Sing "Part of the Family of God." Add this verse. *Preschool Vol. 2* CD track 8, Songbook, p. 15

> I'll thank my great Savior each day,
> I'll share from my heart when I pray.
> My Father above has shown me his love.
> I'll thank my great Savior each day!

☆Let's Make and Pray

Print the following prayer on a large sheet of **poster board**. Hand out **crayons** so the children may draw pictures of themselves praying to God. Then read the prayer aloud.

> Dear Father, we praise you.
> Thank you for sending Jesus to be our Savior. Please forgive our sins.
> Please take care of all your children. Help us to trust and obey you.
> We praise you for your kindness and love. Thank you for listening to us.
> We pray in Jesus' name, Amen.

Jesus healed a crippled woman on the Sabbath.

Luke 13:10–17

Jesus healed a crippled woman on the Sabbath.

Luke 13:10–17

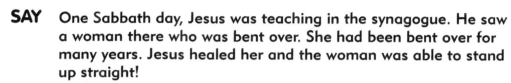

☆ Let's Talk

SAY One Sabbath day, Jesus was teaching in the synagogue. He saw a woman there who was bent over. She had been bent over for many years. Jesus healed her and the woman was able to stand up straight!

ASK *What do you see in the picture?*

SAY The woman praised God for being so wonderful! Many people were glad when they saw what Jesus did and they, too, could not stop praising him.

ASK *What do we learn about Jesus from this miracle he did?*

SAY When Jesus healed the woman, he showed that he is much more powerful than Satan, the enemy of God. The miracle Jesus did shows that Jesus is God and that he has power over everything.

☆ Let's Build and Imagine

Set out **blocks** and **toy people**. Let the children build a synagogue (a Jewish worship center), adding people in the synagogue on the Sabbath. They may show the woman Jesus healed. They may show her and the other people praising God.

☆ Let's Listen, Make, and Sing

❶ Listen to "Jesus, I Love You." Give the children **paper** and **crayons** to draw pictures to illustrate the song. For example, they can draw a heart to represent "love," hands to show "serve," and pictures of themselves singing to illustrate "praise."

Preschool Vol. 2 CD
Songbook, p. 21

❷ Then sing the song together. As you sing, the children may hold up the matching picture they made.

☆ Let's Move and Say

❶ Let children move their bodies in different ways. Have them crouch, do jumping jacks, touch toes, lift arms high, walk around, bend, and so on.

❷ Then have them name ways they use their bodies to do different things. Conclude this activity by thanking God for the bodies he has given us to love, serve, and praise him!

© GCP www.gcp.org
OK to photocopy for church and home use

The shepherd looked for his one lost sheep.

Luke 15:1–7

The shepherd looked for his one lost sheep.
Luke 15:1–7

☆Let's Talk and Wonder

SAY Jesus told the people a story. He said there was a shepherd who had 100 sheep. One day, the shepherd counted his sheep. He counted—one, two, three . . . all the way up to 99. He found that one sheep was missing!

ASK *What do you think might have happened to the missing sheep?*

SAY Sometimes sheep like to wander. Maybe the sheep fell down some big rocks. Perhaps a wolf or lion got hold of the sheep.

ASK *What do you think the kind and loving shepherd did?*

SAY The shepherd went out to look for the one sheep that was lost. When he found it, he was very glad! He carried it safely home. He called his friends and neighbors over. "Be happy with me," he said, "because I found my lost sheep!"

SAY I wonder what Jesus wanted people to learn from this story . . .

SAY Sinners are like the lost sheep in the story. Jesus, our good Shepherd, seeks out, finds, and saves the lost sinner. Everyone rejoices when the one who was lost is found!

☆Let's Make

Make a **photocopy** of the coloring page for each child. Mount it on **poster board**. Provide **cotton** for the children to **glue** onto their sheep. You may also set out **fabric, felt, rice, beans,** and **glitter glue**.

☆Let's Sing and Move

Gather in a circle. Sing "The Lord Is My Shepherd." Include actions such as hopping like lambs and so on.

 Toddler Sing-Along With Me CD Songbook, p. 21

The prodigal son who ran away came home to his father.

Luke 15:11–24

The prodigal son who ran away came home to his father.

Luke 15:11–24

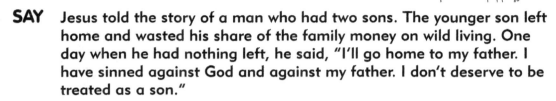

☆Let's Talk

SAY Jesus told the story of a man who had two sons. The younger son left home and wasted his share of the family money on wild living. One day when he had nothing left, he said, "I'll go home to my father. I have sinned against God and against my father. I don't deserve to be treated as a son."

ASK *What do you think the father did when his son returned?*

SAY The father ran to meet his son. He hugged and kissed him and gladly forgave him. The father planned a grand dinner to celebrate his son's return home.

ASK *Why did Jesus tell this story?*

SAY Jesus wanted his followers to understand that God is like the father in the story. Our loving heavenly Father forgives his children because Jesus died for our sins. Those who trust in Jesus as Savior can always go to God the Father for forgiveness. He forgives all our sin and makes our hearts clean!

☆Let's Listen and Show

❶ Gather a **quilt**, a **Bible**, and **objects** listed in bold below.

property	**money**	*ring*	**plastic ring**
pigs	**toy pigs**	*shoes*	**sandals**
pods	**seedpods**	*calf*	**picture of a young cow**
robe	**bathrobe**	*eat*	**play food set**

❷ Sit in a circle on the quilt. Hand an object to each child. Then read aloud the parable found in Luke 15:11–24. Tell the children to listen carefully. As you read, emphasize the key words in italic above that match the objects. Each time you emphasize a word, the child with the matching object will put it in the center of the circle. Afterward, let the children pick up the objects and retell the story.

☆Let's Sing and Pray

Sing "I Am Trusting You, Lord Jesus." Then lead the children in saying this prayer.

Preschool Vol. 2 CD Songbook, p. 17

Dear heavenly Father, please forgive us when we disobey you. Thank you that you forgive us because Jesus died for our sins. Help us to grow in trusting and obeying you. In Jesus' name, Amen.

Luke 15

Jesus healed a lame man at the pool.

John 5:1–15

Jesus healed a lame man at the pool.
John 5:1–15

☆ Let's Talk

SAY Jesus went to the pool of Bethesda in Jerusalem.

ASK Look at the picture. *What did Jesus see there?*

SAY Jesus saw a man lying by the pool who could not walk. Like the other sick, blind, and crippled people there, he waited for the water to bubble up. Everyone believed that the first person to get in the pool when the water moved would be healed of any sickness.

ASK *What do you think Jesus said to the man?*

SAY Jesus asked the man if he wanted to get well. Then Jesus healed him. The man got up, picked up his mat, and walked away. Later on, Jesus saw him at the temple and told the man to stop sinning or something worse might happen to him. Now the man knew that it was the Lord Jesus who had made him well. Jesus is God the Savior. He has power to heal and to forgive sins!

☆ Let's Play

Have the children line up at one end of the room. At the other end of the room, spread a large **blue beach towel or blanket** on the floor to represent the pool of Bethesda. Stand by the blanket to lead *Race to the Pool*. At your command, children try to be the first to get to the pool as they *walk quickly* across the room. Then have them line up once again. Continue the game by calling out a different action. For example, children can *run* to the pool, *jump* to the pool, *tiptoe* to the pool, and so on. Play continues until several or all children have had an opportunity to be the first to reach the pool.

☆ Let's Do and Say

Put a number of **first-aid objects** in a **bag**. Let children take turns pulling an item from the bag and telling what the item is used for. When everyone has had a turn, talk about how Jesus healed people in ways that medicine, doctors, nurses, and parents cannot.

☆ Let's Pray

Dear Lord Jesus, thank you that you have power over everything because you are God. We pray for those who are sick and ask you to help them. Please forgive our sins, and help us to trust and obey you. In your name we pray, Amen.

Many people put their trust in Jesus.
John 8:12–59

Many people put their trust in Jesus.
John 8:12–59

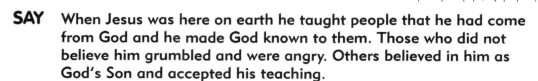

☆ Let's Talk

SAY When Jesus was here on earth he taught people that he had come from God and he made God known to them. Those who did not believe him grumbled and were angry. Others believed in him as God's Son and accepted his teaching.

SAY The Pharisees, who were leaders and teachers of the Law, did not understand what Jesus said. When Jesus explained who he was, they complained. They did not believe he was God's Son. They did not believe he was the promised Savior.

ASK Look at the picture. *What does it show?*

SAY There were other people who gladly believed in Jesus and followed him. Jesus said that he was the Son of God, the promised Savior sent by God to save his people. We also gladly follow him because we believe Jesus our Savior is God's Son!

☆ Let's Act

Have each child who is willing act out being a Pharisee or a follower of Jesus. They can dress up in simple **Bible-times clothing** and show by their actions and facial expressions whether they are angry Pharisees or joyful followers. Let the other children guess the role the child is playing. The correct guesser can be the next one to act!

☆ Let's Sing

Sing together "Believe in the Lord Jesus." Include these additional verses.

Toddler Sing-Along With Me CD (track 19) Songbook, p. 20

❶ He is God the Son,
He is God the Son,
He is God the Son,
Sent from heaven to earth.

❷ Jesus is my Savior,
Jesus is my Savior,
Jesus is my Savior,
I'll gladly follow him.

Jesus cares for his people like a shepherd cares for his sheep.
John 10:1–18

☆ Let's Talk

ASK *What do you see in the picture? How do you think a good shepherd takes care of his sheep?*

SAY A good shepherd gives his sheep food, clean water, and rest. He brings back young lambs that wander off and protects the flock from wild animals. He leads them to the sheep pen at night, where they are safe from harm.

ASK Jesus said that God's children are like sheep and he is their shepherd. *How is Jesus like a shepherd and how are we like his sheep?*

SAY Just as a loving shepherd looks after his sheep, so Jesus takes care of God's people. Jesus gives them everything they need to live, and they listen to his voice and trust and obey him.

SAY Nothing can take us away from Jesus. He died on the cross to save us from our sins, he watches over us each day, and one day we will live with him forever. The Lord Jesus, our good Shepherd, is the best shepherd of all. He takes wonderful care of God's family!

☆ Let's Do an Active Rhyme

Act out the words in italic. Have the children repeat each line after you and imitate your actions.

>*Five* little sheep *sit* by the sheep pen door,
>One *goes in* and now there are *four*.
>*Four* little sheep *hop* around a tree,
>One *skips* away and now there are *three*.
>*Three* little sheep bleat "Baa" and "Boo,"
>One *hides* behind the shepherd and now there are *two*.
>*Two* little sheep *leaping* in the sun,
>One *gets a drink* and now there is *one*.
>*One sad* little sheep is not having fun,
>He *runs* off to the shepherd and now there are none!

☆ Let's Pray

Dear God, thank you that Jesus is our good Shepherd. Thank you that he died for our sins and that he takes good care of us. Please help us to trust and obey him. In Jesus' name, Amen.

© GCP www.gcp.org
OK to photocopy for church and home use

Only one healed leper thanked Jesus.
Luke 17:11–19

Only one healed leper thanked Jesus.
Luke 17:11–19

☆ Let's Talk and Wonder

ASK *How many people are in the picture? What are they doing?*

SAY Jesus healed 10 men who had a skin disease called leprosy. Nine went away to show the priests that they were healed. One man returned to Jesus.

ASK *What did the man do when he returned to Jesus?*

SAY He got down on his knees and thanked Jesus for healing him. The man believed in the miraculous power of Jesus and praised God for all he had received that day. Jesus told the grateful man that his faith had made him well.

SAY I wonder how the man felt after he went away from Jesus . . .
I wonder what we can thank God for today . . .

☆ Let's Sing and Do

Gather the children around you. Lead them as they sing and do motions for the following song to the tune *Mary Had a Little Lamb*.

Preschool Vol. 2 CD

❶ Jesus healed 10 sick men,
Ten sick men, 10 sick men.
Jesus healed 10 sick men,
Praise God for he is good!
(hold up 10 fingers)

❷ One came back to thank the Lord,
Thank the Lord, thank the Lord.
One came back to thank the Lord,
Praise God for he is good!
(hold up one finger)

❸ Jesus cares for you and me,
You and me, you and me.
Jesus cares for you and me,
Praise God for he is good!
(point to others, then point to self)

❹ Jesus is my Savior,
My Savior, my Savior.
Jesus is my Savior,
Praise God for he is good!
(point up, then place hand over heart)

☆ Let's Pray

Lead the children in saying this simple prayer, phrase by phrase.

> Dear God, thank you for taking care of me.
> Thank you for sending Jesus to be my Savior.
> In Jesus' name, Amen.

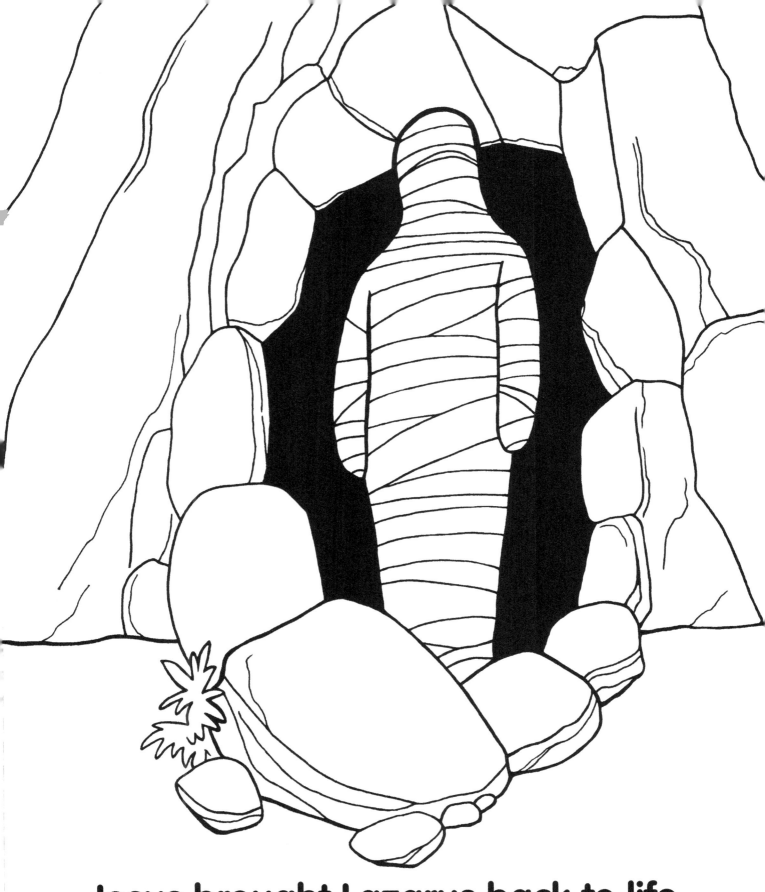

Jesus brought Lazarus back to life.
John 11:1–44

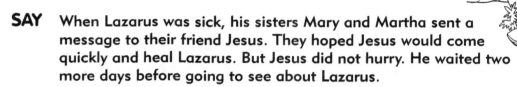

☆Let's Talk

SAY When Lazarus was sick, his sisters Mary and Martha sent a message to their friend Jesus. They hoped Jesus would come quickly and heal Lazarus. But Jesus did not hurry. He waited two more days before going to see about Lazarus.

ASK *What happened when Jesus got to the home of his friends?*

SAY When Jesus and his disciples arrived, they learned that Lazarus had already died. His body had been wrapped in cloths and put in a cave that was his tomb.

ASK *How do you think Mary and Martha felt?*

SAY Mary and Martha were sad that their brother had died. Mary said to Jesus, "Lord, if you had been here, my brother would not have died." When Jesus saw Mary and others crying, he wept also.

ASK Look at the picture. *What do you think happened next?*

SAY They went to the tomb and Jesus said, "Lazarus, come out." Lazarus obeyed because Jesus made him alive again. Many who saw what Jesus did put their faith in him. They believed in the Son of God, sent to save his people from sin and death.

☆Let's Throw and Thank

❶ Before doing the following game, tell the children that Mary and Martha did not stay sad. They were glad when Jesus raised Lazarus from the dead. They were very thankful that Jesus is God's Son, and that he promises to give his people life that lasts forever!

❷ Have the children stand in a circle. You stand in the middle. Toss a **bean bag or ball** to one child. That child will catch it and tell one thing he is thankful to Jesus for. Then he will throw it to another child who does the same. The activity continues until everyone has had a turn.

☆Let's Pray

Lead the children in saying this prayer.

> Dear Lord Jesus, thank your for loving me, saving me, and giving me life that lasts forever. Help me to trust you and follow you always. In your name I pray, Amen.

Mary anointed Jesus with expensive perfume.

John 12:1–8

Mary anointed Jesus with expensive perfume.
John 12:1–8

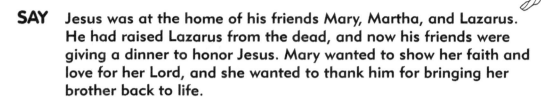

☆Let's Talk

SAY Jesus was at the home of his friends Mary, Martha, and Lazarus. He had raised Lazarus from the dead, and now his friends were giving a dinner to honor Jesus. Mary wanted to show her faith and love for her Lord, and she wanted to thank him for bringing her brother back to life.

ASK Look at the picture. *What do you see?*

SAY Mary brought Jesus an expensive and precious perfume. Mary took the perfume and anointed Jesus' head and feet with the sweet-smelling oil. Using it showed her honor and devotion to Jesus.

ASK *What do you think some people said when they saw what Mary did?*

SAY Judas Iscariot, who later betrayed Jesus, said that Mary should have sold the perfume and given the money to the poor. But Jesus stood up for Mary. He knew that what she did was an act of worship. Mary gave Jesus her time, her attention, her trust and obedience, and the love and devotion of her heart.

☆Let's Show and Tell

❶ Cut out **paper hearts,** one for each child. Have the children draw on the hearts a way to show their hearts overflowing with love and devotion for Jesus. Examples: They can give him their time and attention by listening to Bible stories, learning God's Word, and praying; they can give him their trust and obedience by doing what the Bible says; they can give what they have to Jesus by the things they do, the things they share, the money they give, and so on.

❷ Then gather in a circle. One at a time, have each child hold up his or her picture and tell what it shows.

☆Let's Sing

Sing "Gifts in My Heart" or "O, How I Love Jesus."

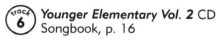
Younger Elementary Vol. 2 CD
Songbook, p. 16

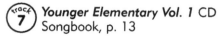
Younger Elementary Vol. 1 CD
Songbook, p. 13

Zacchaeus climbed a tree to see Jesus.

Luke 19:1–10

Zacchaeus climbed a tree to see Jesus.
Luke 19:1–10 (Exodus 20:15)

☆ Let's Talk

ASK *Why did Zacchaeus the tax collector climb a tree?*

SAY Zacchaeus was a short man. He climbed a sycamore-fig tree so he could see Jesus over the crowd of people. When Jesus came by, he stopped and spoke to Zacchaeus. He told Zacchaeus to come down so they could go to his house. The people wondered why Jesus would visit Zacchaeus. No one liked the tax collector because he collected too much money from the people and kept all the extra money for himself. He stole from people, which breaks the eighth commandment.

ASK *Why did Jesus want to spend time with Zacchaeus?*

SAY Jesus loved Zacchaeus and forgave him for his sin. Zacchaeus showed that his heart was changed. He said to Jesus, "I will give half of what I have to the poor. If I cheated anyone, I will pay back four times as much as I took."

☆ Let's Travel

Tell children that in Bible times people didn't have cars to ride in. Instead, they walked, rode on a donkey, or traveled by boat. Pretend to travel as people did in Bible times.

1. **Walk on the road to Zacchaeus's house.** *(children walk in place)*
2. **Ride your donkey to Zacchaeus's house.** *(children walk, bouncing up and down as though riding a donkey)*
3. **Row your boat to Zacchaeus's house.** *(children move their arms in a rowing motion as they walk)*

☆ Let's Pray and Sing

Gather children around you. Lead them in singing this prayer, line by line, to the tune *Jesus Loves the Little Children*.

> Jesus, thank you for your love,
> Please forgive all my sins.
> Change my heart, dear Lord, I pray,
> Help me trust you and obey,
> I come in Jesus' precious name, Amen.

Luke 19

© GCP www.gcp.org
OK to photocopy for church and home use

The people waved palm branches to praise Jesus.
Luke 19:28–38

☆ Let's Talk

SAY Jesus was on his way to Jerusalem. The picture shows that the people waved leafy branches and laid down their coats to honor Jesus.

ASK *What do you think the people said?*

SAY They said, "Blessed is the King who comes in the name of the Lord!" Jesus is God's King, who came to deliver his people from the kingdom of sin and death. He is our Savior and he is our King.

ASK *How can we show that he is our King?*

SAY We show that he is our King when we trust him, praise him, and obey his Word.

☆ Let's Do

1. Seat the children in a circle. Divide the circle in half.
2. Give each child on the left side of the circle a sheet of **brown construction paper**. Explain that the brown paper stands for coats and that the name of their team is *Coats*.
3. Give each child on the right side of the circle a sheet of **green construction paper**. Explain that the green paper stands for leafy branches and that the name of their team is *Leafy Branches*.
4. Tell teams that you will say something from the Bible story. When they hear you say the name of their team, they are to hold up their papers.
5. Say each of the following sentences slowly and give teams time to respond.

- The disciples put their *coats* on the donkey's back to make a saddle for Jesus.
- Jesus sat on the *coats* covering the donkey's back and rode into Jerusalem.
- When the people saw Jesus coming, they began spreading their *coats* along the road.
- Some people cut *leafy branches* from the trees.
- They put the *leafy branches* on the road.
- The people used their *coats* and *leafy branches* to honor King Jesus!

☆ Let's Make and Praise

Outline in large letters **We Praise King Jesus** on a length of **shelf paper** to make a banner. Have the children color the letters and decorate the banner with **glitter glue** and **praise stickers**. Let the children hold up the banner and march around as they say, "We praise King Jesus!"

Jesus cleansed the temple.
Mark 11:15–18

☆ Let's Talk

ASK *What does the picture show?*

SAY When Jesus came to the temple, he saw that it had become a marketplace. Buying and selling didn't belong in God's house because it kept people from worshiping God. So Jesus chased the traders away and turned over their tables and chairs.

ASK *Why could Jesus make things right in the temple?*

SAY Jesus could make things right in the temple because he is God's Son, King Jesus. He had the power and right to bring his Father's house back to its proper use so people could pray and worship God there.

ASK *Can Jesus make things right in our hearts and lives?*

SAY Jesus has the power to make things right in our hearts and lives, too. He saves us from our sins and brings his saving rule into our lives. He changes our hearts so that we can trust him as our Savior and obey him as our loving King!

☆ Let's Sing

Lead the children in singing "God Loved Us, and Sent His Son." Then teach the children this additional verse.

Preschool Vol. 1 CD
Songbook, p. 21

> We're so glad that Jesus is King,
> Let our lips with his praises ring!

☆ Let's Pray

Gather the children. Lead them in saying this prayer, phrase by phrase.

> Dear Jesus, I am helpless without you.
> Show me how to depend on you.
> Thank you for being my Savior and King.
> In your name I pray, Amen.

Jesus washed the disciples' feet.

John 13:1–17

Jesus washed the disciples' feet.
John 13:1–17

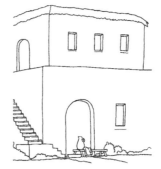

☆Let's Talk

SAY Jesus and his disciples went to a house to celebrate the Passover meal. When they arrived, there was a basin, a pitcher of water, and a towel at the door.

ASK *Why were these things at the door?*

SAY In the time of Jesus, when someone entered a home, water was provided for washing dusty feet. Usually, a servant washed the feet of arriving guests. When Jesus and his disciples arrived, there was no servant to do the work of washing feet.

ASK *What do you think Jesus did?*

SAY Jesus himself washed and dried his disciples' dusty feet. The men were surprised that their Lord would do the work of a servant. Jesus wanted to show them how to serve and he told them they should follow his example. Being great in God's family means humbly helping and serving others.

☆Let's Make and Explore

1. Draw the outline of a cross on a large sheet of **poster board**. Let the children color the cross with **brown crayons**. Then **glue** several **brown craft foam pieces** to the cross to make it stand out and appear wooden.
2. Tell the children that the greatest way Jesus served his people was coming to earth to be our Savior. Jesus, the Son of God, died on a cross to save us. Since Jesus served us by saving us from our sins, we can be glad to humbly serve one another.
3. Explore everyday ways that your children can serve and help others.

☆Let's Rhyme and Show

Stand in a circle. Take turns showing serving actions as you say this rhyme together.

> Serving, serving,
> Everybody, everywhere.
> Serving, serving,
> Everybody do your share!

For example, children can show emptying the trash can, scrubbing the sink, sweeping the floor, cleaning the litter box, and so on. Say the rhyme several times so every child has an opportunity to act out one way to serve.

The disciples received the Lord's Supper.

Luke 22:7–20

The disciples received the Lord's Supper.
Luke 22:7–20

☆Let's Talk

SAY Jesus told his disciples to eat bread and drink wine to remember his death on the cross.

ASK What do you see in the picture?

SAY Jesus was teaching his disciples, and all those who trust in him, that instead of celebrating the Passover meal, we are to celebrate the Lord's Supper. It reminds us that Jesus has paid for our sin, that Jesus rose from the dead, and that one day he will return. When God's people worship him by celebrating the Lord's Supper, it is a joyful time for the church!

☆Let's Do

❶ Draw the outline of a large cross, a plate of bread, and a cup of wine on a large sheet of **poster board**. Talk about what each picture shows.

- The *cross* reminds us that Jesus paid for our sins.
- The *bread* makes us think about the body of Jesus that was crucified on the cross for our sins.
- The *wine* in the cup makes us think about the blood of Jesus that was shed for our sins.

❷ Let children color the pictures. Then they can make touch-and-feel pictures by **gluing** one or more of the following items on the picture: **cotton, rice, strips of tissue paper, glitter, fabric**.

☆Let's Memorize

Gather in a circle. Teach questions 137 and 140, listed below. Say the question and have the children sit as they repeat it. Then say the answer and have them stand as they repeat it.

First Catechism Q/A 137, 140

137 **Q.** *What sign is used in the Lord's Supper?*
A. Eating bread and drinking wine to remember the suffering and death of Jesus.

140 **Q.** *Who may rightly partake of the Lord's Supper?*
A. Those who repent of their sins, trust in Christ, live a godly life, and profess their faith before the Church.

The disciples listened as Jesus told them about the Holy Spirit.

John 14

The disciples listened as Jesus told them about the Holy Spirit.
John 14

☆ Let's Talk

SAY One night, Jesus told his disciples that he was going to leave them soon and go back to his Father. He was going to prepare a home in heaven so that one day all God's family could be with him forever.

ASK Look at the picture. *What do you think the disciples might have said when Jesus told them he was going back to his Father in heaven?*

SAY They might have said, "What will happen to us when Jesus leaves? Who will teach us about God? Who will help us trust and obey? Who will comfort us when we are sad or afraid?"

ASK Jesus told his disciples not to be afraid. He said God would send the Holy Spirit. *What would the Holy Spirit do?*

SAY After Jesus left, the Holy Spirit would come to live in God's people. The Holy Spirit would be their helper and he would be with them always.

ASK *How does the Holy Spirit help God's children?*

SAY The Holy Spirit is God. We cannot see him, but he lives within each person in God's family and gives us the power we need to live for Jesus. He teaches us when we hear God's Word. The Holy Spirit comforts us and makes us strong. He helps us remember God's Word and helps us obey.

☆ Let's Sew

❶ Cut out **large red hearts**, one for each child. Paste each heart on **cardboard**. Use a **hole puncher** to punch holes an inch or two apart around the edge of each heart. At one hole, tie a piece of colorful **yarn** for sewing. Add **tape** around the other end to make for easier threading. Show the children how to thread the yarn in and out of the holes.

❷ As they work, remind children that the Holy Spirit came to change the hearts of people, help them trust in Jesus as Savior, and help them grow in trusting and obeying God.

☆ Let's Pray

Gather in a circle. Lead children in saying this prayer.

> Dear God, thank you for giving your Spirit to each of your children. Thank you that he changes our hearts. Thank you that he helps us grow in trusting and obeying you. In Jesus' name, Amen.

Men came to arrest Jesus.
Luke 22:39–53

Men came to arrest Jesus.
Luke 22:39–53

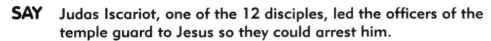

☆Let's Talk

SAY Judas Iscariot, one of the 12 disciples, led the officers of the temple guard to Jesus so they could arrest him.

ASK *Do you know what time of day they came to arrest him?*

SAY It was nighttime. Jesus was arrested in a favorite garden spot on the Mount of Olives where he went to pray.

ASK Jesus is the powerful Son of God. *Why didn't he stop the men from arresting him?*

SAY Jesus knew that the time had come for him to die on the cross. Jesus knew that this was the way he would accomplish our salvation. So Jesus did not stop Judas and the crowd of enemies. He allowed the officers to arrest him and take him away to the house of the high priest. Jesus chose to obey God's will so that we could be forgiven.

☆Let's Walk and Worship

Lead children around the room on an imaginary walk up the Mount of Olives. Stop and "rest" several times along the way. At each stop, encourage one or two children to take turns completing this sentence: **"I love Jesus because. . . ."** Give your young volunteers time to express their praise in their own words.

☆Let's Pray

Teach children this prayer to the tune *Jesus Loves Me*.  *Preschool Vol. 1* CD

Verse
Jesus, you obeyed, I know,
For the Bible tells me so.
You went to the cross for me,
You died, from sin to set me free!

Chorus
I love you, Jesus.
I love you, Jesus.
I love you, Jesus.
I want the world to know!

Peter was sad that he denied Jesus three times.

Matthew 26

Peter was sad that he denied Jesus three times.
Matthew 26

☆ Let's Talk

SAY Jesus told his disciples that soon he was going to die. He said they would all leave him.

ASK *What do you think Peter said?*

SAY Peter said he would never turn away from Jesus. But Jesus said that before the rooster crowed, Peter would deny knowing Jesus three times. Then soldiers came and took Jesus away, and the disciples ran off.

ASK *What do you think Peter did?*

SAY Different people came up to Peter and said that he had been with Jesus. Three times, Peter angrily denied being a follower of Jesus. Then a rooster crowed. Suddenly Peter remembered what Jesus had said. Peter went away and cried. He was very sorry for his sin.

ASK *After Jesus died and rose again, what do you think he said to Peter?*

SAY Jesus said to Peter, "Follow me!" Jesus loved Peter and forgave him. Jesus gave Peter the power to trust him and obey his command. Peter was ready and willing to follow his risen Lord!

☆ Let's Make and Mention

1. Print *I will follow Jesus* on a sheet of **paper**. Make a **photocopy** for each child. Have each child place his or her hands on the paper and trace around them. Some children may need help. Let them color in their traced hands.

2. Explain that the command Jesus gave Peter to follow him is for us as well. And even when we sin, Jesus forgives us when we ask him. Mention ways your children can use their hands to follow Jesus. For example, they can share with others, help others, turn the pages of a Bible storybook to learn more about Jesus, fold their hands in prayer, and so on.

☆ Let's Sing and Pray

Gather in a circle. Sing this prayer to the tune *Jesus Loves Me*.

track 39 Preschool Vol. 1 CD

Verse
Thank you, Jesus, for this day.
Give me power to obey
Your command to follow you,
Forgive me when I sin, I pray.

Chorus
Help me, Lord Jesus,
Help me, Lord Jesus.
Help me, Lord Jesus,
To follow you each day!

Jesus died on the cross.

Luke 23

Jesus died on the cross.
Luke 23

☆Let's Talk and Wonder

ASK *Why did Jesus die on the cross?*

SAY Jesus died on the cross so that our sins could be forgiven.

ASK *Did Jesus deserve to die?*

SAY Jesus never did or said one wrong thing; he did not deserve to die. Jesus obeyed his Father's will for our salvation. He took responsibility for our sins on the cross and submitted to the judgment of God, taking the punishment we deserve.

SAY I wonder what we can say to thank and praise Jesus for loving us and dying on the cross for us . . .

☆Let's Sing

One way we can thank Jesus for dying for us is to sing his praises. Lead children in singing "God Loved Us, and Sent His Son." Sing these additional verses and do the suggested actions.

Preschool Vol. 1 CD
Songbook, p. 21

① Jesus took our sins all away.
Thank the Savior every day!
(form cross with both arms)

② We're so glad that Jesus is King,
Let our lips with his praises ring!
(raise both arms and wave them)

☆Let's Memorize

Go over these questions with your children.

First Catechism Q/A 50, 58

50 Q. *How could Christ suffer?*
   A. Christ, the Son of God, became a man so that he could obey and suffer in our place.

58 Q. *What must you do to be saved?*
   A. I must repent of my sin and believe in Christ as my Savior.

 **A dying criminal turned to Jesus.**
Luke 23:32–43

☆Let's Talk and Wonder

SAY Jesus willingly went to the cross because he came to die for the sins of his people. He hung on the middle cross between two criminals.

SAY I wonder what the two men thought as they hung beside Jesus . . .

SAY One criminal mocked Jesus. "Aren't you the Christ?" he said. "Save yourself and us." The other man said, "We are getting the punishment we deserve. But this man has done nothing wrong." Then he looked at Jesus and said, "Remember me when you come into your kingdom." This man knew he was a sinner. He was asking for mercy. He was asking the Savior for his free gift of salvation.

SAY Jesus turned to him and said, "Truly, I say to you, today you will be with me in Paradise."

SAY I wonder how the criminal felt when he heard what Jesus said . . .

SAY The helpless man must have been filled with peace, knowing his sins were forgiven and he would be with Jesus in his kingdom. He trusted Jesus as his Savior and now he was forgiven! Like the criminal on the cross, we are all sinners and deserve to be punished for our sin. But the good news is that Jesus was punished in the place of sinners. God our Savior saves all those who come to him for forgiveness!

☆Let's Make and Tell

Set out **building blocks**. Encourage the children to build three crosses to represent the crucifixion scene. As they build, children can retell the Bible story.

☆Let's Do, Say, and Pray

❶ Print *We thank God for his mercy* in block letters on a large sheet of **paper**. Let children color the letters.

❷ As they work, mention the fact that we depend on God's mercy and forgiveness every day. God's mercy is his love and kindness to us. We would be helpless without it. Children can mention some of God's gifts to us—family, home, church, friends, and so on. Then talk about God's amazing mercy toward us in sending the Savior.

❸ After coloring and sharing, lead the children in this prayer.

> Dear God our Savior, thank you for your gifts to us that we enjoy every day. Thank you for your amazing kindness and love in sending Jesus. Thank you for saving those who come to you for mercy. In Jesus' name, Amen.

Joseph of Arimathea provided a tomb for Jesus' body.

Matthew 27:57–61

Joseph of Arimathea provided a tomb for Jesus' body.
Matthew 27:57–61

☆Let's Talk

SAY Joseph of Arimathea had become a follower of Jesus. At first, he had been afraid to let people know. But after Jesus died on the cross, he acted boldly. He went to Pilate, the Roman leader, and asked for the body of Jesus. Pilate ordered that it be given to him.

ASK What did Joseph do with Jesus' body?

SAY Joseph carried the body of Jesus away and wrapped it in a clean linen cloth. Then he placed it in his own new tomb. Joseph rolled a big stone in front of the entrance.

SAY But neither the tomb nor the stone could hold the Lord Jesus. On the third day, God raised Jesus from the dead, and his followers saw their Savior with their very own eyes. We can praise God that Jesus our Savior is alive!

☆Let's Construct and Plan

1. Cut **butcher paper** to the approximate height of the children, one sheet per child. Have a helper assist you in tracing around each child as he lies on the floor. Help cut out body outlines. Each child can personalize his outline by adding hair, facial features, and clothing.

2. As children work on their "body-portraits," mention that Joseph of Arimathea loved and served the Lord. Let children mention ways they can love and serve the Lord at home, at school, at church, and where they live.

☆Let's Sing

Sing "Be Strong." The words of the song fit well with the Bible story of Joseph of Arimathea and will encourage the children to ask Jesus to help them tell others about him.

(track 10) *Younger Elementary Vol. 2* CD
Songbook, p. 23

Jesus is alive!

Luke 24:1–12

Jesus is alive!
Luke 24:1–12

☆Let's Talk

ASK Peter went to Jesus' tomb. *What did he see?*

SAY He saw the grave clothes lying where Jesus' body had been. But Jesus himself was not in the tomb.

ASK *Where was Jesus?*

SAY Jesus didn't stay in the tomb because he is God our Savior! He came alive on the third day, just as he promised he would. Later, the risen Savior appeared to Peter and the other disciples. He filled them with trust so they could say joyfully, "The Lord is risen indeed!"

☆Let's Share the Good News

Divide children into two groups. Lead groups in sharing the good news that Jesus is alive. Have the first group ask in unison, **"Where is the Lord Jesus?"** The second group will respond, **"The Lord is risen indeed!"** Then have the groups switch roles.

☆Let's Sing

Lead the children in listening to and singing "We Welcome Glad Easter."

Preschool Vol. 1 CD
Songbook, p. 20

☆Let's Roll and Thank

❶ Remind the children that when Jesus' followers went to the tomb on the third day, they found that the stone in front of the opening had been rolled away. The angels told them that Jesus had risen from the dead. Now show the children a **beach ball**. Roll it across the floor and tell them that when they roll it they can remember the stone that was rolled away.

❷ Have the children sit in a circle. Roll the ball to one child. Have her name something she wants to thank the risen Savior for. Then she rolls the ball to another child. Continue the activity until each child has had a turn to roll the ball and thank the risen Savior.

Mary Magdalene saw Jesus' empty tomb.
John 20:1–18

☆Let's Talk and Wonder

SAY Jesus died on a cross. Then he was buried in a tomb with a stone rolled in front of it. On the first day of the week, Mary Magdalene went to the tomb and saw that the stone had been rolled away. She ran and told Peter and John, Jesus' disciples. When they got to the tomb, they saw that Jesus was not in there, but the grave clothes were lying inside. Peter and John returned home.

ASK Look at the picture. *What did Mary do?*

SAY Mary stayed at the tomb and cried. But then Jesus came and stood by her and called her name. Now Mary knew that Jesus was no longer dead. She was very glad! She ran off to tell the disciples that she had seen the risen Lord!

ASK *What is the greatest miracle of all?*

SAY The greatest miracle of all is that Jesus died and rose from the dead. God loves us so much that he sent his Son, Jesus, to die on the cross to pay the punishment his people deserve for their sins. When Jesus rose from the dead, it showed that he had power over sin and death. Jesus our Savior is alive, and one day those who trust in him will live with him forever!

☆Let's Make

1. Print *Jesus is alive!* in the middle of a sheet of **poster board**. Give children **crayons, scissors, glue,** and **construction paper in pretty spring colors**. Let them draw flowers, birds, butterflies, and bees and cut them out. Children can paste the pastel cutouts around the caption on the poster board.

2. Talk with the children about what it means to trust in the living Savior and tell others the good news about him!

☆Let's Say

Lead the children in saying *The Apostles' Creed* (found in the *Trinity Hymnal*, page 845). Say each sentence or phrase slowly and expressively and let the children repeat the words after you.

Two people talked to the risen Jesus as they walked to Emmaus.

Luke 24:13–35

☆Let's Talk

SAY Cleopas and his friend were walking along a road. They were sad that Jesus had been crucified. The two men talked about all that had taken place.

ASK Then what happened?

SAY Jesus appeared to the two men, but they were not able to recognize him. Jesus began to teach them about the Savior God had promised to send. Jesus explained everything that was written about him in the Scriptures. When they reached the village, Jesus joined them for the evening meal.

ASK When God showed the men that it was Jesus who was sitting there with them, how did they feel and what did they do?

SAY They were very happy because they had just seen the risen Savior! The two men hurried back to Jerusalem to tell the good news about Jesus to his followers gathered there.

☆Let's Eat and Listen

1. Invite the children to sit around the table. Hand out **pita chips or pretzel sticks** (be aware of any allergies).
2. Talk about how we can trust in the risen Savior and tell others about him.

☆Let's Guess

Tell the Bible story. As you tell it, pantomime the action words instead of saying them. The children can try to identify the missing words.

> **Cleopas and his friend were** *(walking)* **and** *(talking)*. **They were** *(sad)* **that Jesus had died. Then Jesus came along. Even though the men did not know it was Jesus who was speaking to them, they** *(listened)* **and** *(nodded)*. **When the men got to the village, they stopped** *(walking)*. **They** *(sat down)* **to eat a meal, and Jesus showed himself to them. Then he disappeared. The two men were** *(happy)*. **They** *(got up)* **and** *(ran)* **to Jerusalem to tell the other disciples. "Jesus is alive!" they said happily.**

The disciples saw the risen Jesus.
Luke 24:36–49

☆Let's Talk

SAY After Jesus died, the disciples were in a house in Jerusalem behind locked doors. Jesus suddenly appeared among his frightened followers. He showed them the marks left by the nails of the cross. Then he ate with them and taught them from God's Word.

SAY He told his followers that he was the Savior promised by God. He explained that he had suffered and died so sinners could be forgiven. By rising from the dead, Jesus gives life to all those who put their trust in the Savior.

ASK *What command did Jesus give the disciples?*

SAY He told them to tell everyone the message of salvation. Jesus said he would send the Holy Spirit to give them power to spread the good news that Jesus saves sinners.

☆Let's Make and Wonder

1 Set out **play dough**. Use it to make simple shapes of some of the people who saw the risen Christ.

2 While making the people, talk about how Jesus appeared to Peter, Cleopas and his friend, and the others. Point out that Thomas, one of the disciples, was not present when Jesus suddenly appeared in the room. But he was with them when Jesus appeared to the group some time later. When Thomas saw Jesus, he believed right away and said, "My Lord and my God!"

3 Spend time wondering how the children can share the good news about the risen Savior with people in their neighborhoods and elsewhere.

☆Let's Pray

Gather in a circle. Lead the children in saying this prayer, phrase by phrase.

> **Dear Jesus, you died on the cross for our sins. You rose from the dead on the third day, just as you said you would. God's Word says that you are the living Savior. Help us to trust in you. Thank you that even though we cannot see you, your Spirit is with us. Help us to tell others the good news about you! In your name we pray, Amen.**

The disciples saw Jesus return to heaven.

Luke 24:50–53

The disciples saw Jesus return to heaven.
Luke 24:50–53

☆Let's Talk

ASK *Who are the men in the picture? What are they doing?*

SAY When it was time for Jesus to return to his Father in heaven, he led his disciples out to the Mount of Olives. He told them that the Holy Spirit would come and be with them, even though they would not see him. The Holy Spirit would give them power to understand and obey God's Word and tell others about the Savior. Then Jesus blessed the disciples, and he was lifted up from them. A cloud hid him from their eyes as they kept looking up. Then they didn't see him anymore.

ASK *How do you think the disciples felt when Jesus returned to his Father in heaven?*

SAY The disciples were joyful! They knew that even though Jesus had gone to be with his Father, his Spirit would be with them wherever they would go.

☆Let's Rhyme

Invite children to stand in a circle. Teach them the following rhyme and have them clap or march in step as they say the words rhythmically.

❶ WE have HEARD
FROM God's WORD—
JEsus CAME to SAVE us!

❷ HE'S God's SON
HE'S the ONE—
HE'S our RISen KING!

❸ Back to HEAV'N he WENT
THEN he SENT—
His SPIrit to LIVE with US!

☆Let's Do

After children have finished coloring the picture, let them **glue cotton balls** to the clouds. Or children can use **cotton swabs** to dab **glitter glue** along the edges of the clouds.

☆Let's Pray

Lead children in this responsive prayer. You will speak first and they will listen to your words. When you stop speaking, they will say, "Help us to trust in you."

Leader: Dear Jesus in heaven, thank you for sending your Spirit to be with us.
Children: Help us to trust in you.
Leader: Give us the power we need to live for you and tell others about you.
Children: Help us to trust in you.
Leader: In your name we pray.
All: Amen.

The disciples received the Holy Spirit at Pentecost.

Acts 1–2

The disciples received the Holy Spirit at Pentecost.
Acts 1–2

☆ Let's Talk and Wonder

SAY Jesus died on the cross and then he rose from the dead. Then he spent time with his disciples. He told them to wait in Jerusalem for the coming of the Holy Spirit. After that, Jesus was taken up to heaven.

ASK Look at the picture. *What do you see?*

SAY Jesus' followers were together in Jerusalem. They heard a noise, like a powerful wind. Then they saw something like a flame of fire resting on each person there. The wind and flames meant that God had sent his Spirit to them. The Holy Spirit had come to live in God's people.

SAY I wonder how the Holy Spirit would help God's people . . .

SAY The Holy Spirit would give them power to trust and obey Jesus. He filled their hearts with joy and they praised God in many different languages. Led by the Spirit, Peter preached about Jesus, the risen Savior, to the crowd that had gathered.

SAY I wonder what the people did when they heard Peter's message . . .

SAY Some of the people were sorry for their sins and asked God to forgive them. That day, many people believed in Jesus and were baptized, and the Holy Spirit came to live in them.

☆ Let's Praise

Tell the children that one way we serve God is by worshiping him when we sing. Let the children play simple **rhythm instruments** as you sing "Trinity" with this additional verse.

Preschool Vol. 2 CD Songbook, p. 28 (track 19)

> Praise the Father, praise the Father,
> And the Son, and the Son,
> And the Holy Spirit, and the Holy Spirit—
> Three in One, three in One.

☆ Let's Make and Say

Print the words *Holy Spirit* on the board or a sheet of **paper.** Let the children copy the words by forming letters out of **play dough.** Mention that just as the Holy Spirit helped Peter preach the good news about the Savior to many people, so the Holy Spirit gives us all we need to live for Jesus and tell others about him.

The disciples obeyed Jesus' command to make disciples.

Acts 1–2

The disciples obeyed Jesus' command to make disciples.
Acts 1–2 (Matthew 28:18–20)

☆Let's Talk and Wonder

ASK *What does the picture show?*

SAY The disciples obeyed the command Jesus gave them. They boldly went from place to place telling others about the Savior.

ASK *What two promises did Jesus give his disciples before he went back to his Father in heaven?*

SAY Jesus promised to send the Holy Spirit to help the disciples trust and obey him, and give them the power they needed to go out and tell others about the Savior. He also promised that one day he would return for all his people with great power and glory.

SAY Jesus' command and promises are not just for the disciples, but also for all of God's children. I wonder what are some ways we can help others learn about the Savior . . .

☆Let's Sing

Lead the children in singing these words to the tune *London Bridge* as they march around the room and do actions.

Preschool Vol. 2 CD

❶ We love Jesus, yes we do,
(cross hands over heart, point up)

Yes we do, yes we do. *(nod)*

We love Jesus, yes we do,
(cross hands over heart, point up)

He's our Savior! *(clap three times)*

❷ We'll share the news with everyone,
(cup hands around mouth)

Everyone, everyone. *(nod)*

We'll share the news with everyone,
(cup hands around mouth)

Jesus is the Savior! *(clap three times)*

☆Let's Name and Pray

❶ Sit in a circle. Let children take turns naming people they want to tell about Jesus. Explain that as God's children keep telling others about the Savior, more people everywhere will know that Jesus died and rose again to save sinners!

❷ Dear Jesus, thank you for being our Savior. Help us to obey your command to tell others about you. We want to share the good news with the people we just named. Thank you that you sent the Holy Spirit to help us obey your commands and believe your promises. We look forward to the day when you will return. In your name we pray, Amen.

Acts 1–2

© GCP www.gcp.org
OK to photocopy for church and home use

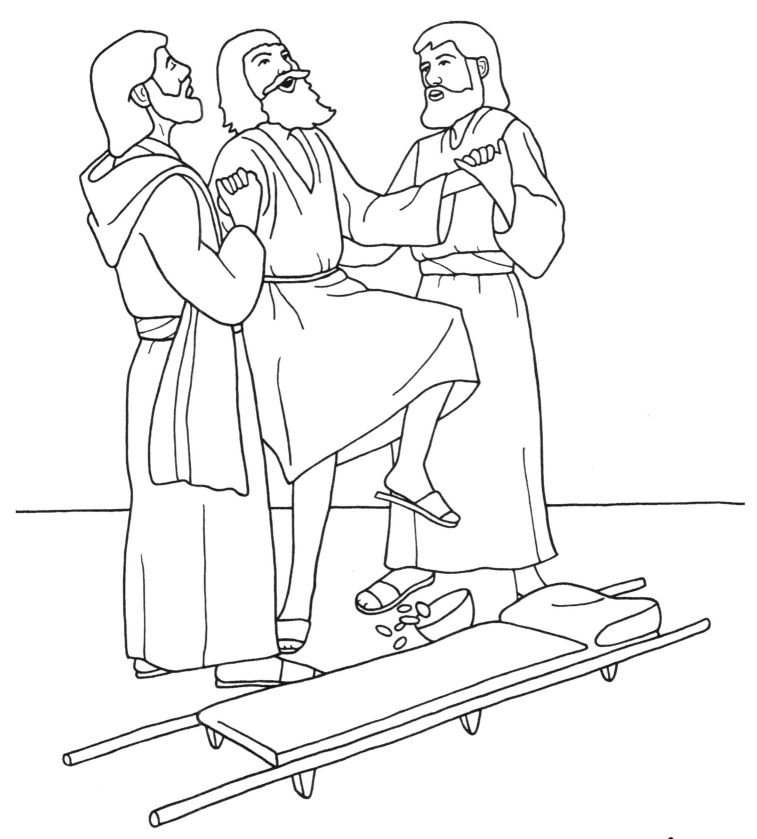

Through Christ's power, Peter and John healed a lame man.

Acts 2:42–3:26

Through Christ's power, Peter and John healed a lame man.
Acts 2:42–3:26

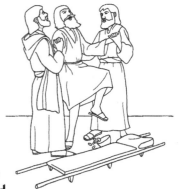

☆Let's Talk

SAY The followers of Jesus studied God's Word, celebrated the Lord's Supper, and prayed together. They ate meals together and shared what they had with those in need. And every day God added more people to his church. One day Peter and John went to the temple and saw a crippled man lying there. He asked them for money.

ASK *What do you think Peter and John did?*

SAY Peter said, "I have no money to give you. But in the name of Jesus Christ of Nazareth, walk."

ASK *What do you see in the picture?*

SAY The man got up and walked. He went with Peter and John into the temple, all the while jumping up and down and praising God. A crowd gathered around them. Peter spoke to the people.

ASK *What do you think Peter said?*

SAY Peter said that it was Jesus that made the crippled man well, not him or John. Peter told the people to turn away from sin. "Turn to God and trust Jesus for forgiveness," Peter said.

☆Let's Draw

1. Tape a length of **butcher paper** to the table. Hand out **crayons** for the children to draw people in the church—pastor, elders, their families, Sunday school teachers, missionaries, and so on.

2. As they draw, remind students that it is God who builds his Church. The Holy Spirit lives in God's people and gives them faith to believe in Jesus, care for one another, and serve the Savior. When they are finished, post the mural on the wall.

☆Let's Pray

Join hands in a circle. Lead the children in this prayer, letting them repeat each sentence after you.

> Dear God, I praise you that Jesus is my Savior. Thank you that the Holy Spirit gives me power to serve you. Teach me how to love you and love others in my church family. In Jesus' name, Amen.

Peter and John told everyone about Jesus.
Acts 4–5

☆ Let's Talk and Wonder

SAY The religious leaders were upset that Peter and John were telling the people about Jesus. They put Peter and John in jail. The next day they asked who gave them power to heal the crippled man.

SAY I wonder what Peter and John said . . .

SAY Peter told the religious leaders that the man was made well by the power of Jesus Christ of Nazareth. Then the religious leaders warned them not to speak or teach in the name of Jesus.

SAY I wonder what Peter and John said . . .

SAY "We cannot stop telling about all God has done," Peter and John said. "We must obey God." The leaders gave them another stern warning, then let them go. After this, Peter and John and the other disciples boldly went out and told everyone about the Savior!

☆ Let's Imagine

Stretch a **sheet or quilt** across a table, shelves, or chairs to represent a prison cell. Let pairs of volunteers take turns pretending to be Peter and John. They can sit inside and talk about Jesus while pretending to spend the night inside a prison.

☆ Let's Do

Do the following fingerplay to emphasize that the Holy Spirit gives us the power and courage we need to serve the Savior.

- **Who gives us courage to serve the Savior?** *(hold hands out, palms up)*
- **Do you know? Do I know?** *(point to others, then point to self)*
- **Who gives us courage to serve the Savior?** *(hold hands out, palms up)*
- **He is God the Holy Spirit!** *(raise both arms)*

© GCP www.gcp.org
OK to photocopy for church and home use

The disciples chose seven godly men.
Acts 6:1–7

The disciples chose seven godly men.
Acts 6:1–7

☆Let's Talk

SAY The church in Jerusalem kept growing. There were some women in the church whose husbands had died. They were called *widows*. They didn't have money to buy food. They needed help. "God has called us to teach his Word and pray," the disciples said. "Choose seven godly men to care for the widows and poor."

ASK *What do you think the seven godly men were like?*

SAY The people in the church chose men who loved the Lord Jesus and were filled with the Holy Spirit. Then Peter, John, and the other leaders prayed for the men.

ASK *How did the seven men serve the church?*

SAY The men who were chosen did the work God gave them to do. They served food to the widows and took care of the poor. Peter and John and those in the church were glad that the needs of God's people were being met. Jesus Christ was building his church through the power of the Holy Spirit, and his church grew some more.

☆Let's Play

Play a game of tag called *Peter and the Seven*. Choose a child to be Peter. He then tries to tag the other children, who are the seven chosen by the Jerusalem church. When a child is tagged, play stops and the child names one way he can serve the Lord Jesus in the church. Then play resumes as before.

When all the children have been tagged and have named a variety of ways to serve, help them understand that God gives *everyone* in the church opportunities to serve him. There are many different jobs that people can do and each job is important.

☆Let's Name and Pray

Help the children name those who have special jobs in the church. Make a list. Then pray for the pastor, elders, deacons, Sunday school teachers, and other workers on your list. Conclude by thanking God for giving *all* his children jobs to do so everything gets done. Ask him for help to do the jobs he gives us.

Philip explained God's Word.
Acts 8:26–40

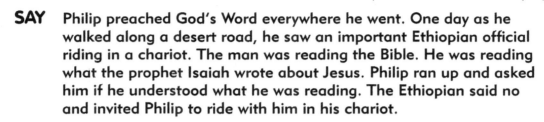

☆Let's Talk

SAY Philip preached God's Word everywhere he went. One day as he walked along a desert road, he saw an important Ethiopian official riding in a chariot. The man was reading the Bible. He was reading what the prophet Isaiah wrote about Jesus. Philip ran up and asked him if he understood what he was reading. The Ethiopian said no and invited Philip to ride with him in his chariot.

ASK *What does the picture show?*

SAY Philip gladly sat with the Ethiopian. He explained that Isaiah was writing about the promised Savior, who came to save sinners. Philip told him that Jesus died on the cross to take the punishment for the sins of all God's people. Jesus rose from the dead and is alive now.

ASK *What did the Ethiopian do when Philip explained the good news about Jesus?*

SAY The Ethiopian believed that Jesus really is the Savior whom Isaiah had written about. As soon as they came to some water, the man asked Philip to baptize him!

☆Let's Roll and Say

Sit in a circle on the floor. Roll a **ball** to someone and say a Bible word from today's story. That child then rolls the ball to another child while saying another word from the story. Keep going until everyone has had a chance to mention a word: *Philip, Ethiopian, Isaiah, chariot, God's Word, Jesus, Savior, sins, good news, believe, Holy Spirit, water, baptized.*

☆Let's Make

1. Find and make a **photocopy of a picture of a Bible** for each child. Help the children **glue** the picture to the middle of a **paper plate**. Set out **scissors** and old **magazines**. Have everyone look for pictures of children to cut or tear out and glue to the plate around the Bible picture.

2. Display the finished Bible collages. *Say* **God wants his children to listen as he speaks to us through his Word. We can ask Jesus to help us understand and believe the Bible, and to help us share the good news with others!**

Dorcas served the church by sewing clothes for the poor.

Acts 9:36–42

Dorcas served the church by sewing clothes for the poor.
Acts 9:36–42

☆Let's Talk

SAY Dorcas loved Jesus very much. She served Jesus by helping others. She did kind things for people in the church. She made clothes for the poor.

ASK *What do you think happened to Dorcas?*

SAY Dorcas became sick and died. Everyone was very sad. The people in the church sent for Peter. He hurried to the room where Dorcas's body lay. Peter got down on his knees and prayed to God. When he was finished, he said, "Dorcas, get up."

ASK *What did God do for Dorcas?*

SAY God brought Dorcas back to life. She opened her eyes and sat up. Peter helped her stand up. All the people were glad because of what God had done! Now Dorcas could continue to serve Jesus by helping others. The news about her spread everywhere and many people came to believe in the Lord Jesus.

☆Let's Make and Mention

Make a **photocopy** of the coloring page for each child. **Glue** it on **poster board**. Provide items to glue onto the pictures: **glitter, felt,** and **fabric** for the robe Dorcas is sewing. As the children work, mention ways to serve others in love at school, church, and home.

☆Let's Sing and Pray

Gather in a circle. Sing this prayer to the tune *London Bridge Is Falling Down*. *Preschool Vol. 2 CD* (track 42)

① Jesus, I belong to you,
Help me serve in all I do.
Jesus, I belong to you,
You're my Savior!

② Help me serve you every day,
Help me serve in every way.
Help me serve you every day,
Thank you, Jesus!

③ Showing love when we serve others,
Friends and family, sisters, brothers.
Showing love when we serve others,
Help us, Jesus!

Peter told Cornelius to believe in Jesus.

Acts 10

Peter told Cornelius to believe in Jesus.
Acts 10

☆Let's Talk

SAY God showed Peter that it was time for him to preach the good news about Jesus to Gentiles as well as to Jews. Even though Jews and Gentiles were different from each other and did not spend time together, Peter did as God told him. He went to the town where Cornelius, a military officer, and his family lived.

ASK *What do you see in the picture?*

SAY Cornelius and his family were Gentiles. But Peter entered his home, where he found everyone waiting to hear the message the Lord had given Peter.

ASK *What did Peter say?*

SAY "God does not have favorites," Peter said. "He has called people from every nation to be part of his family. God sent his Son, Jesus, to be the Savior of Jews and Gentiles. Jesus was nailed to the cross for our sins, but God raised him from the dead. The living Savior told us to spread the good news about him to all the world."

ASK *What happened to Cornelius and his family when they heard about Jesus?*

SAY Cornelius's household believed in Jesus and began praising God. God had saved the military officer and his household, and Peter said they should be baptized in the name of Jesus Christ. Jewish Christians were amazed when they saw God's love and grace poured out on Gentiles. After this, Peter stayed with Cornelius for several days!

☆Let's Play and Pray

1. Print the names of places around the world and near home on separate **index cards**. Give each child a card and make sure he knows the name of the country or region on his card. Sit in a circle.

2. *Say* **We're going to play a game to help us remember places around the world where people live who need to hear about Jesus.** Call out the name of one place and a way to move (skip, tiptoe, baby steps, giant steps, and so on). The child holding the card moves around the circle in the manner called and then returns to her place in the circle. Repeat, naming a different place and way to move until everyone has had a turn.

3. Pray for missionaries who take the message of the gospel everywhere. Ask God to help us love those who are different and share the message of Jesus with them.

Paul and Barnabas brought offerings to the Jerusalem church.

Acts 11:19–30

Paul and Barnabas brought offerings to the Jerusalem church.
Acts 11:19–30

☆Let's Talk and Wonder

SAY The church in Jerusalem sent Barnabas to visit the new church in Antioch. Barnabas asked Paul to come and help him.

ASK *What do you think the two men did there?*

SAY Barnabas and Paul served together in Antioch. They taught the people about the Lord Jesus. The people listened and learned to love and serve God and serve others.

SAY I wonder what the church in Antioch did to serve others . . .

SAY One way the church in Antioch served others was by giving money to the church in Jerusalem to help those who were in need of food.

ASK *What do you see in the picture?*

SAY Barnabas and Paul took the offering to the church in Jerusalem. The people there were thankful for the gift. The Christians in Antioch were glad they could give to those who needed help. They praised God that they could serve him!

☆Let's Mention and Make

❶ Mention ways to tell others about Jesus and ways to give to others in need. For example, we can invite a new friend to Sunday school so he can learn about Jesus; we can help others in need by sharing toys, food, and clothing with them; and so on.

❷ **Glue** each child's coloring page on a larger sheet of **poster board**. Help the children use **scissors** to cut out pictures from old **magazines**, such as pictures of people smiling, hugging, or talking, or pictures of toys, food, or clothing. Glue the pictures around the edge of the coloring page to make a frame. The pictures will remind the children to tell someone about Jesus and give to someone in need this week!

☆Let's Pray

Sit in a circle. Lead the children in saying this prayer.

Dear God, thank you for sending Jesus to be our Savior. Help us tell others about Jesus. Help us to show our love for you by giving what we have to help others in need. Change our hearts so we want to serve you each day. In Jesus' name, Amen.

Acts 11

© GCP www.gcp.org
OK to photocopy for church and home use

The church prayed for Peter while he was in prison.

Acts 12:1–17

The church prayed for Peter while he was in prison.
Acts 12:1–17

☆ Let's Talk

SAY King Herod wanted Peter to stop telling people about Jesus. So King Herod put Peter in prison. Peter was bound with chains and put between two soldiers. There were soldiers guarding the door.

ASK *Why did King Herod put Peter in chains and have soldiers guard him?*

SAY The king did not want Peter to escape!

ASK Look at the picture. *What did God's people do while Peter was in prison?*

SAY God's people, called Christians, served Jesus by praying for Peter. Meanwhile, Peter lay asleep in prison. He was not afraid because God was with him. He knew that God was stronger than the king, the soldiers, and the prison doors.

ASK *What do you think happened next?*

SAY An angel of the Lord came and woke up Peter. The chains fell off, and the angel led Peter past the guards and out of the prison. Peter went to the house where the Christians were praying and knocked on the door. When they opened the door, they were surprised and glad to see Peter. God had answered their prayers! How thankful they were that God had freed Peter so he could keep on telling others about the Savior!

☆ Let's Say and Write

1. Children can use the board to practice making letters and words. Print *p* and *prayer* and *t* and *trust*. Let children say and copy the letters and words.

2. Point out that God wants us to trust him with our prayers and that praying for the needs of others is one way to serve God and serve one another. Have everyone name specific needs to pray for. Write them on the board. Use the list to pray after singing "Make Me a Servant."

☆ Let's Listen, Sing, and Pray

1. Listen to "Make Me a Servant." Next, sing the song together. Then sit in a circle, and have the children fold their hands and close their eyes. Lead them in saying the words of the song quietly as a prayer.

   Preschool Vol. 2 CD track 15, Songbook, p. 24

2. Conclude this activity by praying for the requests listed earlier. Praise the Lord for listening when we pray, and thank him that he always answers our prayers, giving us the best answer!

The church sent out Paul and Barnabas as missionaries.
Acts 13:1–3

The church sent out Paul and Barnabas as missionaries.
Acts 13:1–3

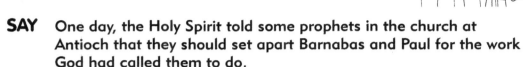

☆ Let's Talk and Wonder

SAY One day, the Holy Spirit told some prophets in the church at Antioch that they should set apart Barnabas and Paul for the work God had called them to do.

ASK *What did God call Barnabas and Paul to do?*

SAY God had called Barnabas and Paul to be missionaries—people who would tell others about Jesus.

ASK *What did the church in Antioch do to set apart Barnabas and Paul?*

SAY When Barnabas and Paul were ready for their trip, the church in Antioch prayed with them and sent them on their way.

ASK *How did Barnabas and Paul feel about being missionaries?*

SAY Barnabas and Paul were glad that God had chosen them to go and tell others about the Lord Jesus. They were glad that the Holy Spirit was with them. He would give them all they needed to spread the good news about the Savior and preach the Word of God!

☆ Let's Listen, Play, and Sing

Provide a variety of **rhythm instruments** for the children to use as they listen to "Let Us Tell Others." Allow them to trade instruments as they listen and play. Then lead them in singing the words.

Preschool Vol. 2 CD
Songbook, p. 27

☆ Let's Find Out and Pray

Do any of the following:

1 Invite a missionary family to visit your class. Have them tell about their work, and also what they do for fun where they live.

2 Set up a missions center. Display pictures of missionaries supported by your church. Put out items such as clothing, toys, money, and crafts from other places around the world where your missionaries serve. Tell the children about the missionaries and let them handle and find out about the items on display.

3 Pray for missionaries. Ask the Lord to provide opportunities for you and the children to tell others about Jesus!

Acts 13

© GCP www.gcp.org
OK to photocopy for church and home use

Paul and Barnabas preached the good news of Jesus.

Acts 13–14

 **Paul and Barnabas preached the good news of Jesus.**
Acts 13–14

☆Let's Talk and Wonder

SAY Paul and Barnabas left Antioch to preach the good news. They traveled from place to place by ship and by land. In one city, they went to the synagogue on the Sabbath day. Paul told the people that God kept his promise to send a Savior. "God sent his Son, Jesus, to die for the sins of his people," Paul said. "Jesus is the living Savior!"

SAY I wonder what the people did when they heard the good news . . .

SAY On the next Sabbath day, a large crowd came to listen to Paul preach. He told the people to believe in the Lord Jesus and be saved. Many put their trust in Jesus.

SAY The new Christians told others about the Savior and the good news about Jesus spread. Meanwhile, Paul and Barnabas continued on their journey. Then it was time for them to return to Antioch. They told the Christians there all that God had done. The church in Antioch praised God that many had put their trust in the Savior.

☆Let's Sing and Pretend

Lead the children in these actions as they pretend to be Paul and Barnabas. Sing to the tune *Here We Go Round the Mulberry Bush*.

track 46 *Preschool Vol. 2 CD*

This is the way we travel by ship,
(pretend to row a boat)
Travel by ship, travel by ship.
This is the way we travel by ship,
So early in the morning.

More verses:
This is the way we travel on land
(walk around the room)

This is the way we spread good news
(make hands into an open book, then raise both arms as if teaching)

This is the way we go back home
(pretend to row a boat again)

This is the way we thank the Lord
(point up, then fold hands in prayer)

☆Let's Pray

Tell the children that we serve God when we remember to pray for those who preach the good news. Say this prayer together, phrase by phrase.

Dear God, thank you for the good news that Jesus is our Savior. Thank you for those who preach the good news, both in our church and around the world. Please give them everything they need to tell others about the Savior. In Jesus' name, Amen.

Lydia believed Paul's gospel message about Jesus.

Acts 16:11–15

Lydia believed Paul's gospel message about Jesus.
Acts 16:11–15

☆ Let's Talk

SAY God sent Paul, Silas, and Timothy to the city of Philippi. On the Sabbath day, Paul and his helpers went down to the riverside where some women had gathered to pray. Lydia, one of the women, had an important business. She sold purple cloth.

SAY Paul and the men sat down and began to speak to the women. Paul told them all about the Savior, the risen Lord Jesus. Lydia's heart was made ready by the Holy Spirit and she trusted in the Lord Jesus as Savior. Lydia and everyone in her household were baptized.

ASK *What do you think Lydia wanted to do now?*

SAY Lydia wanted to serve the Savior. She invited God's servants to her home. She wanted them to have good food and a place to rest. So Paul, Silas, and Timothy stayed at Lydia's house. She took care of them so they had time to tell others the good news about Jesus.

☆ Let's Sing and Move

Sing these words to the tune *The Farmer in the Dell* using actions the words suggest.

Preschool Vol. 2 CD

❶ We use our hands to serve,
We use our hands to serve.
We open them and move them around,
We use our hands to serve.

❷ We use our feet to serve,
We use our feet to serve.
Walking here, there, and everywhere,
We use our feet to serve.

❸ We use our hearts to serve,
We use our hearts to serve.
Reach out and hug a friend!
We use our hearts to serve.

❹ We serve others in love.
We serve others in love.
God gives us the help we need
To serve others in love!

☆ Let's Play and Say

Sit in a circle. Hand a **purple scarf or cloth** to one child. She names one way to show love for others by serving them. Then she gives the scarf to another child. Continue the game until each child has had a turn to name a way to serve and to pass along the scarf. At the end of the game, encourage children to ask Jesus to make them loving servants!

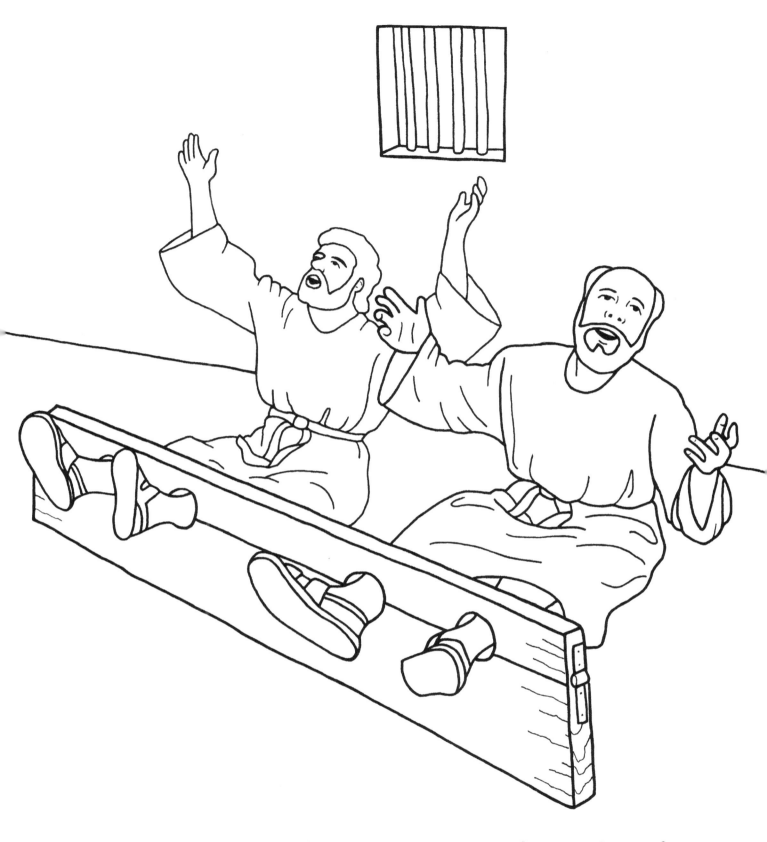

Paul and Silas sang and praised God in prison.

Acts 16:16–40

Paul and Silas sang and praised God in prison.
Acts 16:16–40

☆Let's Talk

SAY Paul went on another missionary journey. This time Silas went with him. In one city, some people wanted to stop the two men from teaching about the Lord Jesus.

ASK *What do you think the people did to Paul and Silas?*

SAY Paul and Silas were beaten and thrown in jail. They were locked in stocks and bonds. But that did not stop them from praying and singing God's praises. The other prisoners and the jailer listened as God's servants prayed and sang.

ASK *What do you think happened next?*

SAY There was a powerful earthquake. Prison doors flew open and the bonds broke loose. The jailer thought everyone had escaped and he was ready to kill himself. But Paul said, "Don't harm yourself. We're all here." The jailer was amazed. He wanted to know what he must do to be saved. Paul told him to believe in the Lord Jesus and he and his household would be saved. The jailer put his trust in the powerful Savior.

SAY The jailer took Paul and Silas to his home. Paul and Silas explained the good news to all the people there. They received Paul's message and were baptized. The jailer and his whole family were filled with joy because he had come to believe in the true God!

☆Let's Make

1. **Tape** a length of **butcher paper** to the wall. Print *We can trust God to help us serve him, even when it is hard* across the top. Hand out **paper** and **crayons**. Let the children draw difficult situations they sometimes face, such as looking for a lost pet, feeling sad because mom is ill, and so on. As they draw, talk about ways to trust Jesus when we are in a difficult situation, such as asking Jesus for help, thanking him that he is with us, thinking about his promises in his Word, and singing songs of praise to him.

2. **Glue** the drawings to the butcher paper. Let the children talk about their pictures.

☆Let's Praise and Pray

Sing "Praise Him." Then gather for prayer. Pray for the children and their concerns. Ask God to give each child a heart filled with love, trust, and obedience. Thank God that his children can always trust him to help them serve him faithfully!

Preschool Vol. 2 CD
Songbook, p. 26

Acts 16

© GCP www.gcp.org
OK to photocopy for church and home use

Paul's nephew warned of Paul's enemies.
Acts 23:11–24

Paul's nephew warned of Paul's enemies.
Acts 23:11–24

☆ Let's Talk and Wonder

SAY The apostle Paul obeyed God's call to preach the gospel to Jews and Gentiles everywhere. Paul went on three missionary journeys, and then he returned to Jerusalem. Some Jews attacked Paul for speaking about the Savior. When an angry crowd gathered, Roman soldiers arrested him and put him in prison.

SAY While Paul was in prison, the Lord told him to have courage. The Lord said that just as Paul had spread the gospel in Jerusalem, he would also go to Rome to preach about Jesus there.

SAY I wonder how Paul felt after the Lord spoke to him . . .

SAY Paul must have been so glad when the Lord encouraged him. Meanwhile, some of Paul's enemies made a plan to kill the apostle. But Paul's young nephew bravely told the Roman commander of the plan, and the commander sent Paul safely on his way guarded by 470 soldiers.

SAY I wonder how Paul's nephew felt when he went to the commander . . .

SAY Paul's nephew might have been scared. But God used Paul's nephew and the commander to protect Paul. God led Paul safely away. Just as God had said, Paul would go to Rome to preach the gospel there.

☆ Let's Make

Talk about what it means to be a helper at home or at school. Then give everyone a sheet of **paper**. Let the children draw pictures of times when they have been helpers. Hand out **scissors** so they can cut out their pictures and **glue** them on a large sheet of **poster board** with these words across the top: *I will be a helper!* Point out that when we help others, it makes them glad.

☆ Let's Sing

Lead the children in singing this prayer to the tune *Here We Go Round the Mulberry Bush*.

track 46 *Preschool Vol. 2 CD*

❶ Jesus, show me how to be
A helper, a helper.
Jesus, show me how to be
A helper every day.

❷ Help me to serve God's people,
God's people, God's people.
Help me to serve God's people,
Each and every day.

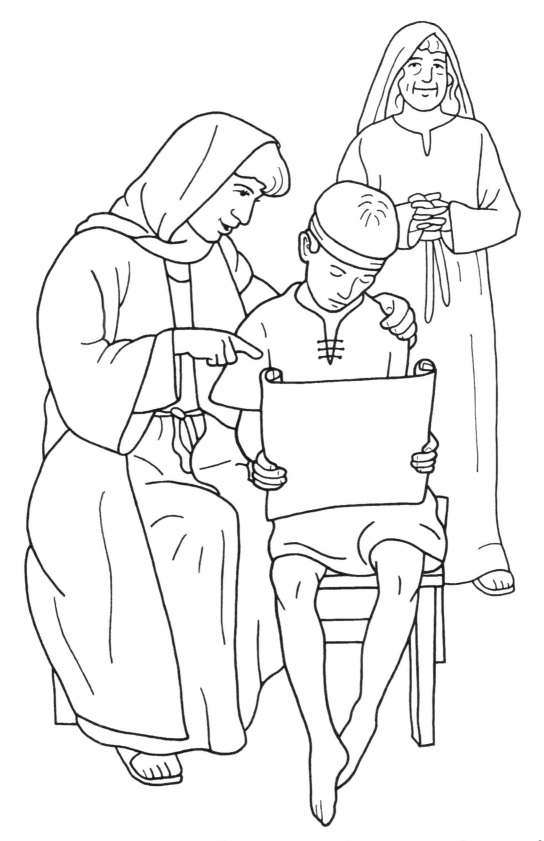

Timothy's mother and grandmother taught him God's Word.

2 Timothy 1:5

Timothy's mother and grandmother taught him God's Word.
2 Timothy 1:5

☆Let's Talk

ASK Look at the picture. *What do you see?*

SAY When Timothy was a young boy, he lived with his mother, Eunice, and his grandmother Lois. Timothy's mother and grandmother loved God. They wanted Timothy to love God also. So they spent time with Timothy, teaching him God's Word.

ASK *As Timothy grew, what did he learn about the Savior?*

SAY Timothy learned that God had promised to send the Savior. Timothy learned that God's promises are in his Word, the Bible.

ASK *What did Timothy grow up to be?*

SAY Timothy became a helper to the apostle Paul. Timothy loved Jesus and he loved God's Word, so he traveled with Paul, teaching people about Jesus. Near the end of Paul's life, God helped Paul write two letters to Timothy. These letters are God's Word and tell us all about Jesus.

☆Let's Find and Say

Have the children close their eyes while you hide the **Bible** somewhere in the room. When someone finds it, the child will name one Bible story, person, or event found in God's Word. Hide the Bible again, and continue playing until several or all of the children have had a chance to find it and name one thing they've learned from the Bible.

☆Let's Memorize and Pray

Teach children the following *First Catechism* question.

> **14 Q.** *Where do you learn how to love and obey God?*
> **A. In the Bible alone.**

Say this prayer.

> Dear God, we praise you for your Word, the Bible. We thank you for those who teach it to us. Please help us hear, learn, and obey your Word when it is read, taught, and explained. Please help us to serve you this week. In Jesus' name, Amen.

2 Timothy 1

© GCP www.gcp.org
OK to photocopy for church and home use

James wrote, "Listen to God's Word and do what it says."

James 1:19–25

James wrote, "Listen to God's Word and do what it says."
James 1:19–25

☆Let's Talk and Remember

SAY God's Word, the Bible, teaches us who God is, what he has done for us, and how we are to love and obey him.

ASK What do you remember about . . .
- Eli the priest, whose sons did not honor God or his Word?
- Ezra, who loved to study, obey, and teach God's Word?
- the prophet Isaiah, who told the people to prepare for the coming of the promised Savior?
- Philip, who explained God's Word to a man from Ethiopia?

SAY God says his Word is true and that it will stand forever. God wants us to listen to his Word and do what it says. God has sent the Holy Spirit to help us listen to his Word, hide it in our hearts, and obey it!

☆Let's Make and Remember

1. Give each child some **play dough**. Have them make a person, place, or thing they remember from a Bible story. For example, they could make a tabernacle, scroll, or chariot. They could shape Eli, Ezra, Philip, or other people. They could form a desert, press out a river, or craft a city.

2. Sit with the children and make something yourself. As you work together, talk about what they are making and how the Bible teaches us about God the Father, Son, and Holy Spirit.

☆Let's Sing

Sing a familiar song that focuses on God's Word, such as "The B-I-B-L-E." Or lead the children in listening to and learning one of the songs about God's Word found in the *Younger Elementary Vol. 1* Songbook or CD (for example, "Open My Eyes" or "Oh, that the Lord Would Guide My Ways").

John wrote a letter to the church that said, "Love one another."
1 John 3–4

☆Let's Talk and Wonder

SAY Long ago, a disciple of Jesus named John wrote a letter to the people in God's family. This letter is in the Bible. We call it First John. The Holy Spirit guided John so he could write what God wanted his people to know and obey. When the letter arrived, God's people listened as John's letter was read to them.

ASK What do you think the letter said?

SAY In the letter, we learn that God showed his love for us by sending his Son, Jesus, to die on the cross for our sins and be our Savior. All those who trust in Jesus are part of God's family. We show love for God by obeying the command of Jesus to love one another.

SAY I wonder what we can do and say to show that we love others . . .

☆Let's Make

1. Make leis. Gather the following: **shoelaces or yarn, small paper hearts, paper flowers,** and **straws** cut in 1-inch pieces. Use a **hole puncher** to punch holes in the middle of the hearts and flowers.

2. Give each child a shoelace and tie a knot at one end. Demonstrate how to thread the paper hearts, flowers, and straws onto the shoelace to make a lei. While working, talk about different things we can do and say to show God's love to others. To complete each lei, tie the ends of the shoelace together.

3. Invite children to try on the leis they made. Encourage them to give them away to show love to someone who needs cheering up. Or you may arrange a group visit to a local nursing home where children can visit residents and give away their leis.

☆Let's Sing

Sing "O, How I Love Jesus." Then sing these additional verses.

Preschool Vol. 2 CD Songbook, p. 17

1. Serve one another,
   Serve one another,
   Serve one another,
   To show that we love the Lord!

2. Love one another,
   Love one another,
   Love one another,
   Jesus says to God's family!

God will make his creation new one day!

Revelation 21:1–4

God will make his creation new one day!
Revelation 21:1–4

☆ Let's Talk and Wonder

ASK *What do you see in the picture? What will happen when God makes his creation new?*

SAY The Bible tells us that when Jesus comes back, all those who trust in the Savior will live with him forever. God will live with his people in the new heavens and the new earth. There will be no more tears or sadness or pain because all the hurt from sin will be gone. Jesus will reign as our king and we will praise him forever!

SAY I wonder how we will feel when we are living with Jesus in our wonderful new home in the new heavens and the new earth . . .

☆ Let's Make

1. Lead your children in making praise tambourines. Bring in **paper plates, colorful stickers, dried beans,** and **streamers.** Give each child two paper plates and show everyone how to turn the plates over and decorate them with stickers and drawings.

2. Then help the children place a handful of beans in one plate, cover it with the second plate, and fasten the edges all around with **staples. Tape** on colorful crepe paper streamers. Make sure children's names are on their tambourines.

☆ Let's Celebrate

Praise God for his goodness and wonderful plan for his people! Listen to "Praise the Lord Our God." Let children shake the tambourines they made as they listen to the song. If they didn't make tambourines, provide simple **rhythm instruments** you have on hand or give everyone **crepe paper streamers** to wave about as they listen and move to the song.

track 4 *Preschool Vol. 1 CD*

Toddler scope & sequence index

Fall Quarter *God's Family*
1. God Created the World 11
2. God Created Adam and Eve 19
3. Adam and Eve Disobeyed God 27, 29, 31
4. God Saved Noah and His Family 37
5. God Promised to Care for His World 37
6. God Gave Abraham a Promise 39
7. God Gave Abraham a Son 43
8. God Gave Isaac a Wife 47
9. God Chose Jacob 49
10. God Cared for Joseph 53
11. God Delivered Joseph 57
12. God Saved Joseph's Family 59
13. God's Promises Give Hope 29, 175

Winter Quarter *God's Son*
1. John's Birth 173
2. The Angel's Visit 171
3. Jesus' Birth 175, 177
4. Simeon and Anna 179
5. The Wise Men 181
6. Jesus in the Temple 183
7. Jesus' Baptism 185
8. Water into Wine 193
9. The Ten Lepers 251
10. The Paralyzed Man 223
11. Blind Bartimaeus 221
12. Jesus and the Fishermen 191
13. Jesus and His Disciples 231

Spring Quarter *God's Love*
1. The Widow's Son 227
2. The Stormy Sea 213
3. Five Loaves and Two Fish 217
4. Jesus' Death 273
5. Jesus' Resurrection 279, 285
6. Jesus' Ascension 287
7. The Good Samaritan 233
8. Mary and Martha 235
9. Jesus Welcomed Little Children 219
10. Zacchaeus 257
11. Following Jesus 247
12. One Lost Sheep 241
13. The Triumphal Entry 259

Summer Quarter *God's People*
1. The Songs of David 115, 117
2. The Birth of Moses 61
3. Moses at the Red Sea 63, 65, 71
4. God Gave Manna 73
5. God Gave Moses the Law 79
6. The Battle of Jericho 97
7. Hannah's Prayer and Praise 107
8. God Called Samuel 109
9. David and Goliath 119
10. Jonah 165
11. Josiah 139
12. Shadrach, Meshach, and Abednego 159
13. Daniel and the Lions' Den 163

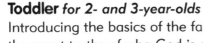

Toddler *for 2- and 3-year-olds*
Introducing the basics of the faith—the vocabulary, the stories, the great truths of who God is and his saving grace through Jesus. CD and songbook also available!

For free samples and to learn more, contact GCP at
www.gcp.org • 800-695-3387

Toddler Curriculum Index

PRESCHOOL Year 1
scope & sequence index

Fall Quarter *God Created All Things*
1. God Created Everything 11
2. God Created Day and Night 13
3. God Created Creatures for Water and Sky .. 15
4. God Created the Earth, Plants, and Land Animals 17
5. God Created Man and Woman 19
6. Tending and Keeping God's World 21
7. God Set Apart the Seventh Day 23
8. God's Covenant of Life 25
9. Sin Spoiled God's Perfect World 27
10. God Reached Out in Love 31
11. God Sent the Savior 29, 273
12. God's Plan for His New Creation 325
13. God Our Creator Is Faithful 151

Winter Quarter *Jesus Is God's Son*
1. God Sends John 173
2. Mary Hears and Believes the Good News .. 171
3. Jesus Is Born 175
4. Simeon Sees the Savior 179
5. Wise Men Worship Jesus 181
6. Jesus Visits the Temple 183
7. John Baptizes Jesus 185
8. Jesus Is Tempted by Satan 187
9. Jesus Visits Nazareth 189
10. Jesus Calls and Makes Fishers of Men 191
11. Jesus Sends Out the Twelve 231
12. Peter Says Jesus Is the Christ 205
13. Jesus Reveals His Glory 207

Spring Quarter *Jesus Is the Savior*
1. Jesus Heals Ten Lepers 251
2. Jesus Blesses Little Children 219
3. Jesus Comes to Zacchaeus's House 257
4. Jesus Enters Jerusalem 259
5. Jesus Cleanses the Temple 261
6. Jesus Establishes the Lord's Supper 265
7. Jesus Is Arrested 269
8. Jesus Dies on the Cross 273
9. Jesus Is Alive 279, 281
10. Jesus Appears to Two Men 283
11. Jesus Appears to His Disciples 285
12. Jesus Returns to Heaven 287
13. Jesus Will Come Again 291

Summer Quarter *God Keeps His Promises*
1. God Gives Adam and Eve a New Son 35
2. God Saves Noah and His Family 37
3. God Calls Abraham 39
4. God Sends Isaac 43
5. God Tests Abraham's Faith 45
6. God Speaks to Jacob 51
7. God Is with Joseph 57
8. God Preserves Jacob's Family 59
9. God Chooses Samuel 109
10. God Sets David Apart 115
11. God Gives David Victory 119
12. God Makes a Promise to David 125
13. God Keeps His Word to Send Jesus 175

Preschool *for 4- and 5-year-olds*
Building on the basics—preschoolers joyfully discover they are part of God's family and that Jesus loves them. CD and songbook also available!

For free samples and to learn more, contact GCP at
www.gcp.org • 800-695-3387

Preschool Curriculum Index

PRESCHOOL Year 2
scope & sequence index

Fall Quarter *God Leads His People*
1. God Takes Care of Moses 61
2. God Calls Moses 63
3. God Sends Moses..................................... 65
4. God Shows His Power............................... 67
5. God Saves His People................................ 69
6. God Leads His People 71
7. God Provides Food 73
8. God Provides Water................................... 75
9. God Keeps His People Safe 77
10. God Makes a Promise 79
11. God Loves and Forgives His Children 83
12. God Is Always Faithful 87
13. God Keeps His Word 93

Winter Quarter *Living in God's Family*
1. God Sends His Son, Jesus....................... 177
2. Jesus Explains Salvation.......................... 195
3. Jesus Cares for His People 249
4. Jesus Promises the Holy Spirit 267
5. Jesus Says, "Pray Like This" 237
6. Jesus Says, "Love God Best" 211
7. Jesus Says, "Love One Another" 323
8. Jesus Says, "Love Your Enemies" 199
9. Jesus Says, "Ask God to Forgive You" 243
10. Jesus Says, "Forgive Others" 209
11. Jesus Says, "Serve Others" 263
12. Jesus Says, "Obey God's Word" 203
13. God Makes Us More Like Jesus 201

Spring Quarter *Jesus Is God*
1. Jesus Changes Water to Wine 193
2. Jesus Calms the Storm 213
3. Jesus Feeds the Five Thousand 217
4. Jesus Heals a Man at the Pool 245
5. Jesus Forgives and Restores.................... 223
6. Jesus Makes a Sick Servant Well 225
7. Jesus Gives Sight 221
8. Jesus Sets a Woman Free 239
9. Jesus Cures Ten Lepers 251
10. Jesus Raises the Widow's Son 227
11. Jesus Gives Life to Jairus's Daughter 215
12. Jesus Brings Lazarus Back to Life 253
13. Jesus Is Alive 281

Summer Quarter *Serving the Savior*
1. Following Jesus 271
2. The Coming of the Holy Spirit................. 289
3. Building God's Church............................ 293
4. Serving the Lord with Courage 295
5. Serving in Different Ways........................ 297
6. Being Taught in God's Word 319
7. Making Our Hearts Ready 313
8. Serving God by Helping Others.............. 301
9. Trusting God in Prayer 307
10. Telling Others and Giving...................... 305
11. Sending God's Servants Out 309
12. Preaching the Good News 311
13. Faithfully Serving the Lord 315

Preschool Curriculum Index

YOUNGER ELEMENTARY Year 1
scope & sequence index

Fall Quarter *Living Together*
1. God Made a Wonderful Home 11
2. God Created People 19, 21
3. Sin Spoiled God's Creation 27, 29
4. We Need God's Forgiveness 35
5. God Saved Noah and His Family 37
6. God Called Abraham 39
7. God Protected Abraham's Family 41
8. God Kept His Promise to Abraham 43, 45
9. God Chose Jacob to Be in His Family 49
10. God Changed Jacob 51
11. God Planned Joseph's Life 53, 57
12. God Used Joseph 59
13. God Still Takes Care of His Family 29

Winter Quarter *Loving Jesus*
1. God Promised to Send the Savior 167
2. Mary Believed God's Message 171
3. Joseph Listened and Obeyed 169
4. The Shepherds Saw Christ the Lord .. 175, 177
5. God Gives Us Power to Repent 185
6. God Gives Us Faith in Christ Alone 257
7. The Holy Spirit Gives New Life 195
8. God Saves Sinners 197
9. Thanking the Lord Jesus 251
10. Giving What We Have to Jesus 255
11. Telling Others about the Savior 191
12. Jesus, God's Son, Gave His Life 273
13. Loving the Risen Savior 279

Spring Quarter *Studying God's Word*
1. God Reveals Himself to Us 11, 13,
   .... 15, 17, 21, 151
2. God's Word Is for His Children 27, 29, 31
3. Eli Failed to Follow God's Word 111
4. King Asa Obeyed God's Word 141
5. Ezra Taught God's Word 147
6. God's Word Is about His Son 153
7. Jesus Loved God's Word 183
8. Jesus Used God's Word 187
9. Jesus Made God's Word Clear 283
10. We Listen to God's Word 299
11. We Learn and Follow God's Word 319
12. God's Word Produces Fruit 201
13. God's Word Lasts Forever 321

Summer Quarter *Growing in God*
1. Knowing God's Plan for His People 61
2. Believing God Loves Us 63
3. Trusting God's Mercy 65, 67, 69
4. Thanking God for His Power 71
5. Depending on God for What We Need 73
6. Learning God's Ways 79, 83
7. Meeting with God 85
8. Learning to Trust and Obey God 87
9. Honoring God's Chosen Leaders 89
10. Thanking God for His Goodness 91
11. Believing God's Promises 95
12. Doing What God Says 97
13. Depending on God Alone 101

Younger Elementary *for 6- and 7-year-olds*
Through stories from the entire Bible, children learn to trust and obey the Savior, building on foundational truths about who God is. CD and songbook also available!

For free samples and to learn more, contact GCP at
www.gcp.org • 800-695-3387

YOUNGER ELEMENTARY Year 2
scope & sequence index

Fall Quarter *Obeying God*
1. Obey God Even When It Is Hard 113
2. God Protects His Children 123
3. God Forgives His Children 127
4. Obey God and Do What Is Right 129
5. Obey God Always 143
6. Trust God and Obey Him 131
7. Trust God and Say What Is Right 133
8. God Is Merciful to Sinners 165
9. Obey God and Be Strong 155
10. Obey a Loving God 157
11. Obey a Powerful God 159
12. Obey a Sovereign God 161
13. Obey a Faithful God 145

Winter Quarter *Knowing Jesus*
1. Getting Ready for the Son of God 173
2. The Coming of Jesus 171
3. A Savior Is Born 175, 177
4. Gifts for the King 181
5. The Early Years of Jesus 183
6. Jesus Faced Temptation 187
7. Having Faith in Christ 193
8. "Let the Little Children Come to Me" 219
9. Believe and Have Life 253
10. "Do You Want to Get Well?" 245
11. Jesus Forgives and Heals 223
12. New Life in Christ 215
13. Jesus Has Power Over Everything 213

Spring Quarter *Serving God*
1. David Relies on God 119
2. Samson Prays for Strength 103
3. Joshua Is Strong and Courageous 99
4. A Servant Girl Trusts God 137
5. God Works through Esther 149
6. Ruth Is a Loyal Servant 105
7. John the Baptist Prepares the Way 185
8. The Forgiven Woman Believes 229
9. A Dying Criminal Turns to Jesus 275
10. Joseph of Arimathea Acts Boldly 277
11. Peter Obeys God's Call 303
12. Paul's Nephew Is Helpful 317
13. Dorcas Is a Faithful Worker 301

Summer Quarter *Pleasing God*
1. God Gives His Law 79
2. Worship God Alone 211
3. Worship God in His Way 83
4. Honor God's Name 63
5. Keep the Lord's Day Holy 81
6. Respect and Obey Parents 111
7. Love and Protect Human Life 33
8. Be Pure in Mind and Heart 55
9. Don't Take What Belongs to Others 257
10. Tell the Truth 135
11. Be Content! 121
12. We Need a Savior 29, 273
13. Jesus Shows Us How to Love 29, 273, 323

Younger Elementary Curriculum Index

BIBLE STORY Index

OLD TESTAMENT

- **Abraham** 39, 41, 43, 45
- **Adam** 19, 21, 23, 25, 27, 29, 31, 33, 35
- **Creation** 11, 13, 15, 17, 19, 21, 23
- **Daniel** 157, 159, 161, 163
- **David** 117, 119, 121, 123, 125, 127
- **Eli** 107, 109, 111
- **Elijah** 131, 133, 135
- **Elisha** 137
- **Esther** 149
- **Eve** 19, 21, 23, 25, 27, 29, 31, 33, 35
- **Ezra** 147
- **Gideon** 101
- **Hannah** 107
- **Isaac** 43, 45, 47, 49
- **Jacob** 49, 51, 53
- **Jonah** 165
- **Joseph** 53, 55, 57, 59
- **Joshua** 87, 93, 95, 97, 99
- **Josiah** 139
- **Lot** 41
- **Moses** 61, 63, 65, 67, 69, 71, 73, 75, 77, 79, 81, 83, 85, 87, 89, 91, 93
- **Naaman** 137
- **Noah** 37
- **Rebekah** 47, 49
- **Ruth** 105
- **Samuel** 107, 109, 113, 115
- **Samson** 103
- **Sarah** 43
- **Saul** 121, 123
- **Shadrach, Meshach, Abednego** 157, 159
- **Solomon** 129

NEW TESTAMENT

- **Barnabas** 305, 309, 311
- **Disciples** 191, 213, 231, 237, 263, 265, 267, 285, 287, 289, 291, 297
- **Dorcas** 301
- **Elizabeth** 173
- **James** 321
- **Jesus, and children** 219
- **Jesus, and followers** 197, 247, 257, 259
- **Jesus, birth and childhood** 169, 171, 175, 177, 179, 181, 183
- **Jesus, death and resurrection** 269, 271, 273, 275, 277, 279, 281, 283, 285, 287
- **Jesus, healings** 215, 221, 223, 225, 227, 239, 245, 251, 253
- **Jesus, miracles** 193, 213, 217
- **Jesus, teachings** 199, 201, 203, 209, 219, 233, 237, 241, 243, 249
- **John** 293, 295, 323
- **John the Baptist** 173, 185
- **Joseph** 169, 171, 175, 177, 179, 181, 183
- **Lydia** 313
- **Mary** 169, 171, 175, 177, 179, 181, 183, 193
- **Mary and Martha** 235, 253, 255
- **Mary Magdalene** 281
- **Nicodemus** 195
- **Peter** 205, 271, 293, 295, 303, 307
- **Philip** 299
- **Paul** 305, 309, 311, 313, 315, 317
- **Silas** 315
- **Timothy** 319
- **Zacchaeus** 257

Curriculum for All Ages!

Show Me Jesus is Bible-based, Christ-centered curriculum that teaches the unfolding story of redemption from Genesis to Revelation and builds on God's truth in age-appropriate ways.

For free samples and to learn more, contact GCP. www.gcp.org • 800-695-3387

Bible Story Index